Advance Praise for

Creating Understanding

"Gasiorek and Aune brilliantly tackle the Communication discipline's most central yet (ironically) most misunderstood problem: how is it that we do this thing we call communication? *Creating Understanding* has totally changed my understanding of understanding. This insightful work is a must read for those interested in the social science of communication."

—Timothy R. Levine, Author, *Duped: Truth-Default Theory and the Science of Lying and Deception*; Professor, University of Alabama at Birmingham

"Understanding is often as difficult to define as it is to experience. How do we understand others, and how do we *know* we have understood them? These are among the provocative questions deftly unpacked in this exciting new volume by Gasiorek and Aune. The authors introduce a process model of how people generate entrainment in their mental representations of interaction. By situating understanding at the core of communication—and by integrating perspectives from philosophy, linguistics, and cognitive psychology—Gasiorek and Aune have reconceptualized the very nature of what it means to understand."

Kory Floyd, Co-editor, *The Handbook of Communication Science and Biology*; Professor, University of Arizona

Creating Understanding

Language as SOCIAL ACTION

Howard Giles
General Editor

Vol. 23

The Language as Social Action series
is part of the Peter Lang Media and Communication list.
Every volume is peer reviewed and meets
the highest quality standards for content and production.

PETER LANG
New York • Bern • Berlin
Brussels • Vienna • Oxford • Warsaw

Jessica Gasiorek and R. Kelly Aune

Creating Understanding

How Communicating Aligns Minds

PETER LANG

New York • Bern • Berlin

Brussels • Vienna • Oxford • Warsaw

Library of Congress Cataloging-in-Publication Data

Names: Gasiorek, Jessica, author. | Aune, R. Kelly, author.
Title: Creating understanding: how communicating aligns minds /
Jessica Gasiorek, R. Kelly Aune.
Description: New York: Peter Lang, 2021.
Series: Language as social action; vol. 23 | ISSN 1529-2436
Includes bibliographical references and index.
Identifiers: LCCN 2020031573 (print) | LCCN 2020031574 (ebook)
ISBN 978-1-4331-6813-0 (hardback) | ISBN 978-1-4331-6815-4 (paperback)
ISBN 978-1-4331-8376-8 (ebook pdf) | ISBN 978-1-4331-8377-5 (epub)
ISBN 978-1-4331-8378-2 (mobi)
Subjects: LCSH: Interpersonal communication. | Communication—Psychological
aspects. | Comprehension. | Interpersonal relations.
Classification: LCC HM1166 .G47 2021 (print) | LCC HM1166 (ebook) |
DDC 302—dc23
LC record available at https://lccn.loc.gov/2020031573
LC ebook record available at https://lccn.loc.gov/2020031574
DOI 10.3726/b17801

Bibliographic information published by **Die Deutsche Nationalbibliothek.**
Die Deutsche Nationalbibliothek lists this publication in the "Deutsche
Nationalbibliografie"; detailed bibliographic data are available
on the Internet at http://dnb.d-nb.de/.

To our families

Table of Contents

Acknowledgments

There are many important people that have contributed to this book, directly and indirectly. We thank the Series Editor, Howie Giles, for his helpful comments and suggestions for improving and refining this text, as well as Marko Dragojevic for his questions and comments on earlier versions of core chapters. We also thank Richard Huskey for his invaluable feedback and time discussing content related to cognitive science and communication neuroscience, and for directing us to resources on these topics. Earlier versions of some of the material in this book were also presented as conference papers (Aune & Gasiorek, 2019; Gasiorek & Aune, 2019), and we appreciate the feedback from peer reviewers we received on those iterations of our work.

We are grateful to our colleagues in the Department of Communicology at the University of Hawai'i at Mānoa for supporting the creation of undergraduate and graduate classes on creating understanding. They embraced the arguments that creating understanding should be central to the educational experiences we provide our majors and graduate students. We also thank the hundreds of students in our classes over the past decade that worked with us as we developed the material for this book. Material in this book incorporates and further expands text from an Open Educational Resource we developed for one of these courses (Gasiorek & Aune, 2017), the creation of which was supported by a grant from the University of Hawai'i at Mānoa's Outreach College.

JG would like to express her appreciation to Howie Giles, Linda Putnam, Scott Reid, and Rene Weber for teaching her how to see the world through the lens of scientific theory, and how to ask and answer questions rigorously and systematically. She also thanks Karen Nylund-Gibson for introducing her to Bayesian statistics.

Finally, we thank our families and friends for their support and encouragement. RKA thanks his sons Brian, Alex, Nathaniel, and Kenny for their patience with his tendency to answer questions with lectures. They never complained—eye rolls perhaps, but no complaints. RKA would also like to acknowledge his spouse and colleague, Krystyna, and remind her—once again—that "all good things come from you."

JG thanks her spouse Jack for his giving her time on weekends and early mornings to write and edit, particularly during a challenging stretch of pandemic stay-at-home orders without childcare (a few months before this manuscript was due). She is also grateful to her mother Joan, for her patience with a lifetime of questions and for fostering a love of learning. Finally, JG would like to thank her daughter Kira—who was born partway through the process of writing this book—for giving her a new appreciation for how humans communicate, entrain, and share the world with one another.

References

Aune, R. K., & Gasiorek, J. (2019, November). *Five thousand years of studying communication: In search of square one.* Paper presented at the National Communication Association Annual Convention, Baltimore, MD.

Gasiorek, J., & Aune, R. K. (2017). *Message processing: The science of creating understanding.* Honolulu, HI: University of Hawai'i at Mānoa Outreach College. Retrieved from: http://pressbooks.oer.hawaii.edu/messageprocessing/

Gasiorek, J., & Aune, R. K. (2019, May). *Toward an integrative model of communication as creating understanding.* Paper presented at the International Communication Association Annual Conference, Washington D.C.

Introduction

In this brief introduction, we describe the origins of this book and its primary goals: to offer an explicit conceptualization of understanding, and to offer insight into the process of creating understanding in human communication. We outline why this is an important topic for communication researchers, and offer a brief sketch of contemporary interdisciplinary scholarship on understanding. We conclude with an outline of this book.

We (the authors) are both communication scholars by training; not surprisingly, we have pursued this path because we are interested how communication works. As a field, communication has great breadth, spanning from the fine arts to neuroscience. We are quantitative social scientists; as such, we represent, and work in a narrow slice of the field's wide span, which we will refer to as the *discipline* of communication[1]. Looking across the considerable body of theoretical and empirical work in communication, we were both struck, and surprised, by the lack of research in our discipline on understanding, and how people come to understand each other.

We came to this question from different backgrounds. One of us (JG) pursued an undergraduate degree in foreign languages (French and Italian), and spent time living and working in France and Belgium before pursuing graduate work in communication. In this, she spent countless hours trying to master new communicative systems, and struggling to express herself—and have others recognize what she intended to express—using those systems. Living abroad, where multilingualism (with varying degrees of proficiency) was the norm, she regularly watched people negotiate what language they would agree to use for an interaction. She also watched people employ a range of creative strategies when their language proficiency presented an obstacle to expressing their ideas. (She also used her own share of these strategies herself). All of these experiences put the process of creating understanding front and center in her everyday life, and rendered it something that could not be taken for granted. When she pursued graduate studies in communication—where she ultimately focused on studying communication accommodation—she was surprised (and honestly, a bit confused) to find that the discipline had relatively little insight into how people create understanding, and related issues.

The other (RKA) found his way to the question of creating understanding without the challenges and benefits of traveling abroad. In graduate school, as a student of human communication, RKA was drawn to studying how people learned implicitly, and how they processed information in non-analytical ways. He was particularly interested in how people communicated successfully using incomplete utterances. In graduate coursework outside his home department, RKA was introduced to scholarship in linguistics and philosophy, where he found scholars addressing these issues. As a faculty member, his research eventually narrowed to what he came to think of as creating understanding, including developing a theory addressing how people assess responsibility for creating understanding in communicative interaction (Aune et al., 2005). Over time, he developed a class that focused solely on how people create understanding in interaction. When JG arrived in the department, RKA happily discovered a colleague that was interested in questions of understanding, and the discussions that ultimately led to this book began in earnest.

Wanting to learn more about understanding, but finding little in our disciplinary home, we looked to our social scientific neighbors and beyond, and found serious inquiries, and insights, into this topic in research from cognitive sciences, psychology, linguistics and philosophy. However, and not surprisingly, scholars in each of these fields addressed these questions through their own disciplinary lens. They focused on different aspects of the process, and approached the question at different levels of abstraction.

Reading this work was illuminating, but no single source captured the process of creating understanding in a way that we, as communication scholars, were seeking. We also wanted to bring the insights that these other sources provided back to our colleagues in the discipline. As scholars and teachers of communication, we felt that our discipline's lack of engagement with the topic of understanding was a significant—indeed, critical—omission. These sentiments, and the path they ultimately took us down, were the impetus for this book.

Why Understanding Matters

So, one might ask, does our discipline's lack of engagement with understanding matter? An omission is not in and of itself problematic; sometimes a topic or concept receives minimal attention because it is not important or interesting (Davis, 1971). We believe that the question of how people create understanding matters very much, and is both important and interesting.

From a theoretical perspective, this topic is foundational: the creation of understanding underlies many of the other outcomes that communication scholars study. For example, when interpersonal communication researchers examine the role of disclosure in developing and maintaining relationships (e.g. Taylor & Altman, 1987), there is an implicit assumption that people understand the content of each other's disclosures (if not, simply making sounds and/or being in the presence of another person should be sufficient to build a relationship). Similarly, persuasion researchers assume that people process and comprehend the content in persuasive messages that researchers craft and test, and that this processing and comprehension of message content underlies message effects. There are also many areas of communication research that address understanding implicitly or indirectly (see Chapter 1 for a more extended discussion of this point). This collective body of work would likely benefit from having a consistent theoretical foundation.

For empirical social scientists, the topic of creating understanding also has important methodological implications. At present, most empirical work in the discipline of communication (and indeed, we would argue, in our neighboring social scientific disciplines as well) takes for granted that research participants understand the instructions they are given, and that they understand the communicative stimuli researchers employ. When studies involve interaction, researchers assume that participants (and sometimes, confederates) understand each other. It is standard practice to include memory checks or manipulation checks to ensure that participants recall what they were exposed to, and that a stimulus had the effect that was intended. However, this approach does not necessarily confirm that participants *understood* the message they encountered as the researcher intended—it simply shows that the message was recalled, or it had the desired effect. (For a discussion of related issues with manipulation checks in persuasion research, see O'Keefe, 2003). As a discipline, communication has not clearly theorized how people come to understand each other, or how people comprehend the messages they encounter. Without a theoretical compass that orients researchers to this topic, it becomes easier to overlook in the practices that guide study design and execution.

Finally, from a practical perspective, knowing how people (effectively) create understanding is useful and valuable. There are a range of contexts where ensuring comprehension of specific content is important. Communicating information about risks, explaining health-related diagnoses and treatment (e.g. how often to take medication, at what dosage; Burgers et al., 2015), or providing warnings relating to personal safety are just a few of many possible examples (e.g. Gasiorek & Aune, 2017). Closely related, teaching and learning—activities that are central to people's growth, development, and daily lives—essentially consist of creating understanding via communication. Knowing how the process of creating understanding works should allow people to troubleshoot and fix problems more efficiently and effectively across these contexts (or at the very least, have the satisfaction of knowing why something is happening, even if they cannot change it).

Contemporary Scholarship on Creating Understanding

There is a significant body of contemporary scholarship related to how people create understanding; however, it comes from scholars, theorists, and researchers outside the discipline of communication. In what follows, we provide just a few examples.

In the mid-20th century, philosophers Grice (1975, 1989) and Searle (1969) advanced theories that began to look at how communicators found more meaning in utterances than could be explained by a surface analysis of the utterances. *Speech acts theory* (Searle, 1969) offered insight into how utterances that appear to be of one functional form—for example, a statement or an assertion—are intended and (successfully) interpreted as another functional form—for example, a question. Grice's (1975, 1989) ideas about conversational implicature and his *cooperative principle* explained how communicators are able to infer more than is literally stated in many utterances.

Researchers in pragmatics (a sub-field of linguistics addressing language use in context) and linguistic anthropology have also made important contributions to this topic. Sperber and Wilson's (1995) *relevance theory* provided an alternative explanation for how communicators construct and make sense of utterances that appear superficially incomplete or irrelevant. Sperber and Wilson's work is situated at the intersection of pragmatics and cognitive psychology. Additionally,

Levinson and colleagues (e.g. Enfield & Levinson, 2006; Levinson, 2006) have written extensively on language, cognition, and human social interaction, and argued for fundamental similarities in human interaction across a range of languages and cultures.

Much of the work done on understanding comes from the disciplines of psychology and/or cognitive science. Clark, Fussell, and Krauss (e.g. Clark, 1996; Clark & Brennan, 1991; Fussell & Krauss, 1989, 1991) have all contributed to theorizing about the knowledge, beliefs, and assumptions that communicators share in interaction (i.e. *common ground*) and its role in creating understanding. Pickering and Garrod (2004, 2006, 2013) have theorized about the nature of dialogue and comprehension as processes of coordination and alignment at multiple levels. Finally, Scott-Phillips (2015) and colleagues have incorporated theory and research from evolutionary theory and evolutionary psychology into the study of human communication.

More recently, neuroscientific research has provided insight into the brain activity that underlies social interaction (e.g. Lieberman, 2013) and communication (e.g. Hasson et al., 2012; Stephens et al., 2010). This work provides a window into communication, and understanding, at a different level—that is, that of observable biological activity—than previous empirical and theoretical work.

Not surprisingly, scholars from these different areas approach the topics of communication and understanding in different ways, and from different angles. As a result, they provide insights into different aspects of these topics, and do so at different levels of abstraction and granularity. For instance, the conceptual work of Searle and Grice provides a starting point for conceptualizing understanding, as well as insights into the range of ways that communicative behavior can function pragmatically (e.g. as different speech acts). Relevance theory offers a potential explanation for how people arrive at particular inferences, or mental states, based on their interlocutors' communicative behavior, and how people select what communicative behavior to exhibit for a given interlocutor. Pickering and Garrod's (2004, 2013) models emphasize alignment as a key outcome of successful communication, and offer explanations (some of which contrast with relevance theory) for how communicators achieve a state of alignment in interaction. Research on grounding provides insights into how people interactively monitor and address what is or is not perceived to be understood in conversations. Finally, neuroscientific research offers a window into the physiological substrates (i.e. brain activity) that underlie human communication (including many of the interactive activities referenced in other models).

However, no single source offers a satisfying, physiologically grounded, end-to-end explanation of both what understanding is and how people manage to achieve it across a variety of different kinds of interactions. The literature that comes the closest (e.g. Pickering & Garrod, 2013; Sperber & Wilson, 1995) focuses heavily on conversation—and thus, language—which we believe is an important part of the story, but not the whole story. Additionally, much of this work does not actually address *creating understanding* explicitly or directly, despite offering important observations and insights into the process.

This Book

In this book, our aim is to provide an integrative discussion of how people create understanding in interaction, through the process of communication. As communication scholars, we focus this discussion at the level of the dyad—that is, concentrating on a system of two people—though we address other possible interactional configurations. In contrast to much (although not all) of the extant scholarship we draw on, we aim to place *creating understanding* at the theoretical center of this discussion, focusing on the connections between the process of communication and understanding as a state experienced by communicators.

We begin the book with a more detailed discussion of our perspective, approach and aims. We also provide a summary of current interdisciplinary scholarship on the topics of communication and understanding (Chapter 1). We then introduce and explain concepts we will draw on, and offer a conceptualization of *understanding* as entrainment, or alignment, of communicators' mental models of an interaction (Chapter 2). Next, we present a set of foundational observations about human cognition in which we ground subsequent explanations (Chapter 3). In the following chapter, we outline key components of human social interaction, including how people initiate interaction, how people orient and attend to each other's contributions, and how the stimuli people present activate *meme states* (mental representations) (Chapter 4). We then articulate a theoretical model of how people create understanding. In this, we propose that when people communicate, they construct, test, and refine mental models of a joint experience on the basis of the meme states activated by social stimuli. We explain how this can result in the alignment of mental models—that is, understanding—when all parties in an interaction engage in this process in good faith (Chapter 5). In the next chapter, we discuss contextual factors that can influence how people create understanding, including features of the interactional context, the communication medium, communicators' goals, and social and cultural norms (Chapter 6). We then address how codification relates to understanding, and how communicative systems emerge in interaction as a result of efforts to create understanding

(Chapter 7). In the book's penultimate chapter, we discuss how the perspective and model we introduce complement and connect to other, extant concepts and theories in the discipline of communication, including theories of interpersonal and intergroup communication and deception. We also discuss the theoretical and methodological implications of our framework (Chapter 8). Finally, we conclude with a summary of the contributions and limitations of the framework we propose, with an eye to future directions for research (Chapter 9).

Note

1. Although the terms "field" and "discipline" are often used interchangeably, we use "field" to refer to the broader collective of arts, humanities, and sciences that have communication as their common area of interest, and "discipline" to refer to the subgroups of artists, scholars, and scientists who identify themselves with specific, narrow, and cohesive ontological and epistemological approaches to studying communication. In this book, we will use the term "discipline" to refer to social and natural science approaches to studying communication.

References

Aune, R. K., Levine, T. R., Park, H. S., Asada, K. J. K., & Banas, J. A. (2005). Tests of a theory of communicative responsibility. *Journal of Language and Social Psychology, 24*(4), 358–381. https://doi.org/10.1177/0261927X05281425

Burgers, C., Beukeboom, C. J., Sparks, L., & Diepeveen, V. (2015). How (not) to inform patients about drug use: Use and effects of negations in Dutch patient information leaflets. *Pharmacoepidemiology and Drug Safety, 24*(2), 137–143. https://doi.org/10.1002/pds.3679

Clark, H. H. (1996). *Using language.* Cambridge University Press. https://doi.org/10.1017/CBO9780511620539

Clark, H. H., & Brennan, S. E. (1991). Grounding in communication. In L. B. Resnick, J. M. Levine, & S. D. Teasley (Eds.), *Perspectives on socially shared cognition,* (pp. 127–149). American Psychological Association. https://doi.org/10.1037/10096-006

Davis, M. S. (1971). That's interesting! Towards a phenomenology of sociology and a sociology of phenomenology. *Philosophy of the Social Sciences, 1*(2), 309–344. https://doi.org/10.1177/004839317100100211

Enfield, N. J., & Levinson, S. C. (Eds.). (2006). *Roots of human sociality: Culture, cognition and interaction.* Berg.

Fussell, S. R., & Krauss, R. M. (1989). The effects of intended audience on message production and comprehension: Reference in a common ground framework. *Journal of Experimental Social Psychology, 25*, 203–219. https://doi.org/10.1016/0022-1031(89)90019-X

Fussell, S. R., & Krauss, R. M. (1991). Accuracy and bias in estimates of others' knowledge. *European Journal of Social Psychology, 21,* 445–454. https://doi.org/10.1002/ejsp.2420210507

Gasiorek, J., & Aune, R. K. (2017). Text features related to message comprehension. In R. Parrott (Ed.), *Oxford encyclopedia of health and risk message design and processing.* Oxford University Press. https://doi.org/10.1093/acrefore/9780190228613.013.303

Grice, H. P. (1975). Logic and conversation. In P. Cole & J. Morgan (Eds.), *Syntax and semantics* (Vol. 3, pp. 41–58). Academic Press.

Grice, H. P. (1989). *Studies in the way of words.* Harvard University Press.

Hasson, U., Ghazanfar, A. A., Galantucci, B., Garrod, S., & Keysers, C. (2012). Brain-to-brain coupling: A mechanism for creating and sharing a social world. *Trends in Cognitive Science, 16*(2), 114–121. https://doi.org/10.1016/j.tics.2011.12.007

Levinson, S. C. (2006). On the human "interaction engine". In N. J. Enfield & S. C. Levinson (Eds.), *Roots of human sociality: Culture, cognition, and interaction* (pp. 39–69). Berg.

Lieberman, M. D. (2013). *Social: Why our brains are wired to connect.* Broadway Books.

O'Keefe, D. J. (2003). Message properties, mediating states, and manipulation checks: Claims, evidence, and data analysis in experimental persuasive message effects research. *Communication Theory, 13*(3), 251–274. https://doi.org/10.1111/j.1468-2885.2003.tb00292.x

Pickering, M. J., & Garrod, S. (2004). Toward a mechanistic psychology of dialogue. *Behavioral and Brain Sciences, 27*(2), 169–190. https://doi.org/10.1017/S0140525X04000056

Pickering, M. J., & Garrod, S. (2006). Alignment as the basis for successful communication. *Research on Language and Computation, 4*(2–3), 203–228. https://doi.org/10.1007/s11168-006-9004-0

Pickering, M. J., & Garrod, S. (2013). An integrated theory of language production and comprehension. *Behavioral and Brain Sciences, 36*(4), 329–347. https://doi.org/10.1017/S0140525X12001495

Scott-Phillips, T. C. (2015). *Speaking our minds: Why human communication is different, and how language evolved to make it special.* Palgrave Macmillan.

Searle, J. R. (1969). *Speech acts: An essay in the philosophy of language.* Cambridge University Press. https://doi.org/10.1017/CBO9781139173438

Sperber, D., & Wilson, D. (1995). *Relevance: Communication and cognition (2nd Ed.).* Blackwell.

Stephens, G. J., Silbert, L. J., & Hasson, U. (2010). Speaker-listener neural coupling underlies successful communication. *Proceedings of the National Academy of Sciences, 107,* 14425–14430. https://doi.org/10.1073/pnas.1008662107

Taylor, D. A., & Altman, I. (1987). Communication in interpersonal relationships: Social penetration processes. In M. E. Roloff & G. R. Miller (Eds.), *Interpersonal processes: New directions in communication research* (pp. 257–277). SAGE.

CHAPTER ONE

Communication and Understanding

This chapter addresses the relationship between communication and understanding, in the context of contemporary communication scholarship. Understanding is a topic that communication scholars have largely ignored; we suggest this is a likely a product of the discipline's history, which we briefly summarize. We then review the key features of "code models" of communication, which have dominated disciplinary theoretical and empirical research in communication, and explain their shortcomings. Finally, we argue that our discipline needs a theoretical framework that addresses understanding as its primary focus, and outline how we believe this should be undertaken.

This book is about how people create understanding through communication. Creating understanding is only one of many things that people do when they communicate, we readily acknowledge. However, we contend that it is one of the most fundamental. Most of the other things people do with communication—for example, influence or persuade; make people happy or sad; build or extinguish relationships; define and maintain group boundaries—follow understanding, or are in some way built on understanding as a foundation. However, in the discipline of communication, the construct of understanding has received surprisingly little direct attention from scholars.

There are many topics, constructs and theories in contemporary social scientific communication research that address understanding indirectly. For example, media effects research offers theories describing how people process and arrive at conclusions about the messages they encounter in mass media (e.g. Geise & Baden, 2014; Lang, 2000, 2017), which can include comprehending the content of those messages. In health communication research, patients' variable understanding of medical terminology and information has received considerable attention (e.g. Desme et al., 2013; Majerovitz et al., 1997). Health communication research also addresses how different features and types of messages relate to people's understanding of health-related issues (Mazor et al., 2010) and risks (e.g. Stone et al., 2015). Scholarship on sarcasm, irony, and metaphor examines how these forms of language are interpreted, and by extension (mis)understood, by recipients (e.g. Thompson & Filik, 2016). Miscommunication and misunderstanding—which are clearly related to understanding—have received considerable attention from various angles in interpersonal and intercultural communication research (e.g. Coupland et al., 1991; Sillars, 1998; Sillars et al., 2005), and appear in research on humor (e.g. Buijzen & Valkenberg, 2004).

However, across these bodies of work, communication researchers generally treat "understanding" as a primitive term; it is rarely defined or otherwise probed. Likewise, these bodies of work do not draw on any kind of shared or unified theoretical foundation that explicitly addresses what understanding is, and how it is created. This is likely because the discipline of communication lacks theories that focus on understanding. Most widely used introductory theory textbooks in the field (e.g. Griffin et al., 2019; West & Turner, 2018) do not offer any dedicated scientific theories focusing on how people create understanding in social interaction. Instead, the majority of contemporary scientific theorizing and research in the discipline of communication addresses other outcomes, such as social influence, persuasion, interpersonal relationships, group and organizational dynamics, and media effects.

Origins of an Omission

We believe this state of affairs is likely a result of the discipline's history. The discipline's core areas of research, and the graduate and undergraduate courses reflecting that research, were not developed through a mindful deliberation of what a discipline of communication ought to be. Rather, they emerged somewhat organically, with roots in a variety of disciplinary traditions (Berger, 1991). The task of comprehensively delineating the discipline's history has been undertaken elsewhere (e.g. Delia, 1987), and we do not seek to repeat or reinvent it here. Rather, we wish to briefly highlight some key elements of this history to help shed light on why it has not seriously engaged with the topic of understanding.

Modern social scientific communication research dates to the early part of the 20th century (Delia, 1987). Through the middle of that century, research on communication was generated by scholars from a variety of disciplines, including psychology (e.g. Bateman & Remmers, 1941; Droba, 1931; Festinger, 1957; Murphy, Murphy & Newcomb, 1937; Osborn, 1939), sociology (e.g. Lazersfeld & Stanton, 1949; Mead, 1934; Park, 1940), and journalism (e.g. Lippman, 1922; Nafziger, 1937). The emergence of communication technologies in the early to mid-20th century (e.g. telegraph, telephone, film, radio, television) propelled an interest in media and mass communication that subsequently shaped the emerging field.

With these new technologies came questions about their effects; answering these questions, using the tools of social science, became a major area of focus for communication researchers. A key feature of this work, Delia (1987) highlights, was an interest in how media, messages, and features of the recipient affected *responses* to messages (our emphasis). Researchers generally did not examine whether or how these messages were comprehended. Rather, they were interested in the effect of these messages on people's attitudes and behaviors. Thus, influence, rather than understanding, became a dominant focus of social scientific communication research.

As part of this work on media and media effects, models of communication were developed. Most of these models had their origins in Shannon and Weaver's (1949) model of digital communication (which we discuss further below). Across the decades that followed, communication scholars amended and expanded Shannon and Weaver's model to address additional variables they observed influencing human communication. Examples of such derivative models include those by Schramm (1954) and Berlo (1960).

In the latter half of the 20th century, interpersonal communication emerged as a research area. With this initially came increased interest in how human communication worked, and an interest in further developing and improving extant models of communication (e.g. Miller & Steinberg, 1975; Watzlawick et al., 1967/2011). However, these derivative models generally did not explicitly or directly address understanding. Instead, their focus was on communication as a process of sending and receiving messages, a depiction of communication that retained the essence of a digital communication (i.e. signal-processing) model.

From the 1980s onward, researchers addressing interpersonal communication gravitated toward studying topics addressing the outcomes and effects of communicating (e.g. relationship development and dissolution, love, intimacy, social support, self-disclosure rules and norms, conflict, and deception), rather than the process of communication itself. Today, textbooks and introductory courses in interpersonal communication do address the nature of communication as a process (e.g. Knapp et al., 2014); however, it is generally approached as a spring-board to discuss other topics, rather than a topic of interest in and of itself. In the limited time and space that the nature of communication is given in courses and textbooks, the concept of understanding receives minimal attention.

In short, due to a confluence of different factors and dynamics, the con-temporary discipline of communication never came to see understanding, and the process by which people create it, as focal topics for scholarly investigation. For decades, there was a background hum in the primary journals of the disci-pline that reflected some scholars' concerns that the discipline should be defined more mindfully. If this had been undertaken, someone might have pointed out that scholarship on understanding was conspicuously absent. However, to date, communication researchers have generally allowed the discipline to evolve in a *grounded* manner (e.g. Angus & Lannamann, 1988; Berger & Chaffee, 1987; Wiemann et al., 1988). This grounded approach has led to context-based lines of research and courses such as interpersonal, small group, organizational, and health communication (Berger & Chaffee, 1987; Rains et al., 2020), rather than lines of research and courses addressing shared, underlying processes in communication.

We propose that as a result of this history, communication researchers have been overlooking a fundamental process—if not *the* fundamental process—in our alleged domain of expertise. We also believe that the process through which peo-ple create understanding—which is taken for granted in so much of contemporary communication scholarship—is something communication researchers should investigate. As a starting point for this, the discipline needs a clearly articulated conceptualization of *understanding*, and a framework that explains how people create it. In this book, we seek to offer some initial steps toward these goals.

Classic "Code Models" of Communication: The Problems

With these goals in mind, we now turn our attention to how researchers have his-torically modeled communication. Most of the discipline's contemporary models of communication depict communication as a process of "sending" and "receiving" messages using coded signals or symbols. Sperber and Wilson (1995) have termed this category of models "code models", because the mechanism than enables com-munication is shared "codes" (or symbol systems) such as language.

The basic logic of a code model is that thoughts or ideas (i.e. mental represen-tations) cannot actually travel across time and space, because they are conceptual abstractions, and do not have a physical form. However, if they are converted into something that has a physical form, then this *signal* (i.e. set of physical stimuli which stand for the mental representation of interest) can travel. If an entity can convert the physical signal back into a conceptual abstraction at its destination, then this allows thoughts or ideas to "travel." To be able to reliably convert or translate mental representations into signals, and signals into mental representations, *codes*—that is, systems that reliably pair signals with mental representations—are required.

According to the code model, communication occurs via *encoding* and *decoding* of messages. In this process, senders *encode* their thoughts into signals. This signal is then transmitted through some kind of medium from Point A to Point B, across space and time. During the transmission process, the signal can be distorted, disrupted, or otherwise affected, meaning that the signals that are received at a destination may not be identical to what was sent from a source. Assuming some kind of signal arrives, a receiver *decodes* the message back into thoughts, using the same code that the sender initially used. If this process is successful, then the receiver will end up with the same thought, or mental representation that the sender had at the start of the process. In other words, one person's mental representation will have effectively "traveled" from one point to another. These models essentially position communication as a form of signal processing, a depiction that can be traced back to their origin, Shannon and Weaver's (1949) model of digital communication. In a code model, *understanding* is (implicitly) seen as the result of successful encoding, transmission, and decoding.

Several important assumptions are implicit in the code model. First, as its name suggests, this model treats codes as essential to communication. In the code model, codes are the means by which mental representations (as conceptual abstractions) can be converted into and out of messages. Second, and following from this, this model relies on the application of systematic associations as the primary mechanism by which communication occurs (i.e. using "entries" in a shared code book). This leads to a third assumption: the key skill or ability required to communicate is representing and applying associations. Any entity that can reliably associate signals with corresponding conceptual abstractions, following a set of clearly defined rules (i.e. a code, which pairs them together), should be able to communicate effectively. Accordingly, the "meaning" of a message—that is the ideas or thoughts encoded in a physical signal—is relatively stable and fixed. Thus, a message's form and meaning should be clearly and reliably linked, through the code used to create the message. As such, "meaning" can be seen as a property of a message.

A final, implicit assumption of the code model is that senders and receivers perform their respective operations—encoding and decoding—independently of each other. Because codes are established systems that provide reliable associations between signals and their "meaning", senders and receivers do not need each other to figure out what a signal "means", as long as they both know the code being used. As a practical consequence of this, there is no theoretical problem with researchers focusing on one person, or role (i.e. sender or receiver), at a time when studying communication processes. Thus, this model allows, and to an extent encourages, treating the individual as the primary unit of analysis in research.

Intuitively, code models are appealing; at first glance, they seem to capture what people do when they communicate. However, a closer examination reveals a number of flaws, which scholars have pointed out over the last several decades (e.g. Scott-Phillips, 2015; Sperber & Wilson, 1995). Most importantly, its critics argue that the code model cannot fully explain much of everyday communication, particularly face-to-face interpersonal interactions. Although the model easily describes and explains how a person would interpret a literal statement (e.g. "It is cold in here" to mean, "The temperature is low in this location"), it does not do as well explaining how people successfully create understanding using non-literal or indirect statements (e.g. "It's cold in here" to mean, "Please close the window"). If the primary means by which people share meaning is through a code, it is difficult to explain how people manage to successfully decode non-literal or indirect messages, as their intended meaning does not directly correspond to what is "coded" into the words that speakers use.

Many scholars have sought to address this issue within the paradigm of the code model. For example, some have suggested that we comprehend metaphors, which are one type of non-literal statement, by first processing the literal meaning and then searching for an alternative when the literal meaning does not fit the context (e.g. Clark & Lucy, 1975). However, empirical work has challenged this model of metaphor comprehension, suggesting that people can and do access the meaning of a metaphor directly, often aided by contextual information (e.g. Gildea & Glucksberg, 1982; Wilson & Sperber, 2012). Some have argued that this kind of processing explanation still could, conceivably, be seen as consistent with the code model, if particular code "entries" are accessed differentially in different contexts. However, a mechanism for determining or enabling differential access is then needed. The need for such extra steps to create a viable explanation for non-literal meaning suggests that these situations do not fit cleanly within a code model's framework.

Similar problems arise when one attempts to explain situations where people successfully communicate using ambiguous signals, or stimuli—that is, stimuli that do not necessarily have one (or more) clearly delineated mental representation(s) associated with them. Behaviors such as shared glances, smiles, sighs, or gestures frequently fall in this category: the same facial expression or bodily action can have a wide variety of different "meanings" in different situations. Indeed, a signal such as a pointing finger can "mean" so many different things (e.g. "look at that", "watch out for that", "I think you would find this interesting", "the object you are seeking is here", "this is the problem", "this is the solution") that it would be difficult to argue that the stimulus can be clearly linked to a manageably finite set of concepts or ideas. People use such behaviors quite frequently in their daily lives, however, and a vast majority of the time, they are unremarkable and unproblematic in interaction. However, the code model struggles to explain how people manage to understand each other in these circumstances.

Another situation that the code model struggles to explain is how people interact when they do not share a common code. Consider, for example, a situation in which two people who do not speak the same language try to communicate. (Anyone who has ever travelled to a country or region where they did not speak the local language has likely had this experience). Although they do not initially have a code to rely on—which, according to the code model, is required for successful communication—they are often able to create understanding well enough for their purposes. How do people manage this? In some cases, interactants may be able to switch from their "default" code (e.g. native language) to another code that is shared with their interlocutor (e.g. second or foreign language; use of conventional gestures). For example, someone who speaks Japanese (but not Tagalog) and someone who speaks Tagalog (but not Japanese) might be able to have a conversation in English if they both know English as a second language. Through this adjustment, they are able to create a situation in which a common or shared code becomes available. However, this kind of adjustment is not always an option. When it is not, people often use ambiguous nonverbal stimuli (e.g. gestures, facial expressions, pointing at objects) to try to express and share their thoughts with others. This then returns us to the scenario we considered in the previous paragraph—communicating using ambiguous stimuli—which is sometimes possible, but usually not easy, to explain in terms of the code model.

A final, related criticism of the code model is that it cannot adequately explain situations where people use instantaneous conventions, or improvise, to communicate. Instantaneous conventions are communicative practices (established by usage) that are generated "on the spot" in an interaction (Misyak et al., 2016). Because they are not formalized or set before an interaction, the associations between mental representations and stimuli in such conventions are generally flexible: the same stimulus can be used to indicate one or more different mental representations (e.g. thoughts, ideas), both within and between conversations. For example, waving one's hand in a particular way might be used to indicate, "open the window" in one instance; later in the conversation, the same motion might be used to indicate, "close the window." In a study by Misyak and colleagues (2016), the researchers set up a computer game in which players—who could not see or talk with each other—had to work together to open boxes containing rewards, and avoid opening boxes that contained punishments. One player knew what was in each box but could not open them; the other player had a digital tool to open boxes, but did not know what was in each box. Depending on the resources available for communication and the configuration of rewards and penalties in the boxes in different rounds, the players were observed using the *same signal* (e.g. placing a digital token on a box) to indicate (a) "open this box" and (b) "do not open this box."

This kind of communicative behavior is very difficult to explain with the code model, which relies on stable associations between mental representations and stimuli to explain how meaning is shared via signals. Indeed, a code in which the same signal (e.g. a hand wave) could indicate two opposite meanings (e.g. *both* "open" and "close") is not very helpful or useful for communicating, if that code is the only means people have to create understanding. That people use instantaneous conventions (as well as use more established conventions in novel and flexible ways) in trying to create understanding, and that they do so successfully, suggests that there must be more to human communication than the code model depicts.

In short, we can see that a code model does not offer a satisfactory picture of how human communication works; indeed, it fails to adequately explain many everyday communicative experiences. However, we contend that this does not necessarily make the model wrong or inaccurate. It is just incomplete as a model of human communication; it is only able to explain communication in a subset of situations. First, as its name would suggest, a code model works when there is an established, shared code used by all communicators. Second, this model works for direct and/or literal statements, because they can be encoded and decoded with minimal ambiguity. These qualities generally characterize "well-posed problems": tasks or situations that have a clear "right" answer that one can arrive at by systematically applying sets of rules. However, the code model does not work as well for situations where there is not a shared, established code, stimuli are ambiguous, or signals are being improvised. These qualities generally characterize "ill-posed problems": problems that do not have a clear "right" answer that one can determine or calculate using sets of pre-defined rules. In short, the code model appears to work reasonably well for well-posed (communicative) problems, but not for ill-posed problems. For better or for worse, much of human communication behavior involves negotiating ill-posed problems. Thus, the processes outlined in the code model need to be either augmented or reconsidered to be able to describe and explain the wide range of situations and experiences that constitute human communication.

We propose that conceptualizing human communication in terms of the code model, alongside other elements of the discipline's history (see above), has influenced the way researchers study communication. To date, a majority of research studies looking at human communication have been designed to examine the thoughts and behaviors of one person at a time. Researchers tend to study communicative situations characterized by communicators in clearly defined and relatively static roles as "senders" and "receivers", often with limited feedback between them. If researchers are interested in message construction, they focus on the thoughts and actions of the "sender" or message source. If researchers are interested in message effects, they focus on the thoughts and actions of "receiver", or message target/audience. In either case, the researchers' unit of analysis is the individual. This way of studying communication has been termed a *monologic* approach, because it focuses on what one person at a time is doing or thinking (Pickering & Garrod, 2006).

This is the discipline's dominant approach to studying communication, at present. In addition to the discipline's history and code model conceptualizations of communication, there are also other factors that have perpetuated this state of methodological affairs. First and perhaps foremost, this approach is convenient: focusing on just one individual at a time is much easier than two or more. Second, and related, many of the methods and tools that communication researchers use are oriented toward analyzing static quantities, with the individual as the unit of analysis. Conventional psychological and communication research methods produce outputs such as Likert-type scales assessing attitudes or beliefs, or behaviors that are quantified via coding procedures. (The situations in which these data are collected may be experimental or observational, but the outputs are the same: individual-level, static quantities). Basic inferential statistics (e.g. general linear models), which is what most quantitative social science students are trained to use, allow for comparisons between static quantities, and assume independence of observations, rather than interdependence.

Examining more than one interactant at a time, and looking at how interactants affect each other over time, requires dyadic (or more generally, clustered) data, and/or data collected across multiple time points. To be able to analyze such data appropriately involves more advanced statistical techniques such as multilevel modeling, time series models, or autoregressive models. These are not currently "standard" training for scholars in the discipline of communication, so many researchers are not well versed in these techniques, unless they have gone out of their way to pursue additional statistical training.

If communication is conceptualized in terms of a code model, studying communication using a monologic approach is not intrinsically problematic, and could even be seen as logical. As described above, a code model assumes that communicators can and do engage in encoding and decoding independently, so examining each of these processes independently is reasonable. And indeed, in domains such as oratory or mass communication—which were major areas of focus in the discipline's formative decades—communicative events involve considerable separation in space and/or time between the sending and receiving of a message. In these cases, focusing exclusively on the activities of a "sender" or "receiver" in a given study is reasonable.

However, just as a code model only adequately describes a subset of communicative experiences, a monologic approach to studying human communication is only adequate for investigating a subset of communicative experiences. Specifically, it is a passable approach for situations where communicators are actually processing communicative stimuli independently from each other—for example, when separated in time and space, without the opportunity for any kind of interaction. But in many communicative situations, this is not the case. Interpersonal communication is often face-to-face, dynamic, synchronous, and fluid with respect to sending and receiving; people are generally "sending" and "receiving" simultaneously. Here, it is neither logical nor unproblematic to examine communicators independently: their behavior and cognitions are interdependent.

An alternative to a monologic approach to studying communication is a *dialogic* approach, which examines what happens to two (or more) people interacting together (Pickering & Garrod, 2006). A dialogic approach directs attention to the ways in which people's actions and cognitions affect each other as they interact. In this work, the researchers' unit of analysis is the dyad or group (in the case of interactions involving more than two people). By studying what happens to all individuals involved in a communicative exchange together, researchers can get a picture of how interactants influence each other in the process of communicating, and creating understanding (e.g. Hari & Kujala, 2009; Pickering & Garrod, 2004). In this book, we take a dialogic approach to examining the process of communication and how people create understanding—while acknowledging that there may be situations where a more monologic focus may be reasonable (according to contextual circumstances and researchers' interests in empirical investigations).

Communication as Creating Understanding

Having discussed the pitfalls with how researchers have historically modeled communication, we would now like to articulate our perspective on conceptualizing communication, and the relationship between communication and understanding. Etymologically, the word "communicate" comes from the Latin word "communicare", which means to "share" or "make common". (This is the same word root as "communal", "community" and "common"). Thus, etymologically, when people *communicate*, they are sharing, or *making* something *common*. More specifically, we will argue, they are making thoughts "common", or shared, between communicators. Whenever people seek to communicate—for example, when one person gives directions to another, when a professor is explaining a complex phenomenon to her students, when a parent is explaining the ramifications of a child's behavior to the child—there is a situation characterized by the need to bring one person's thought processes in line with another.

Certainly, there are many situations in which people's primary (or conscious) goal in an interaction is something other than just sharing their thoughts. Social interaction is a goal-directed activity, and people can and frequently do have a wide range of goals beyond "communicating" in the narrow sense we have defined here. For example, people may wish to persuade, influence, express respect, provide social support, or deceive; indeed, in some cases, people may wish to actively prevent others from knowing, or thinking, what they are thinking. However, we contend that even in situations like these examples—in which other goals predominate—there is a fundamental, underlying process that entails communicators' aligning (or subverting alignment of) their thoughts with one another. (The role of communicators' goals in both communication and creating understanding is discussed in greater depth in Chapter 6).

Viewed this way, communication is an inherently dyadic process. It takes two (or more) to communicate, and the defining feature of the process—assuming it is successful—is creating a state in which thoughts or ideas are shared in common. This conceptualization distinguishes communication from related constructs such as *interpretation* or *meaning-making*. We conceptualize interpretation and meaning-making as individual-level processes: they address how people process incoming stimuli, and what conclusions they arrive at as a result. Communication is dyadic: it entails the alignment of two (or more) people's thoughts (though these thoughts may include interpretations of the stimuli presented by the other communicator; see Chapter 2).

In this text, we will focus our discussions and theorizing on *ostensive* human communication—that is, communication in which interlocutors make manifest their intentions to communicate something specific (Sperber & Wilson, 1995). Focusing on ostensive communication, and making the distinction between interpretation as an individual-level process and communication as a dyadic process, we reject the popular perspective that "one cannot not communicate" (Watzlawick et al., 1967/2011). We would argue that, given humans' inherently social nature (see Chapter 3), it might be reasonable to say that "one cannot not process social stimuli and make inferences from it" (which is much less catchy, we admit). However, people can—and frequently do—not ostensively communicate.

Our conceptualization of *understanding*—which we sketch in broad strokes here, and define more precisely in the next chapter—follows directly from defining communication as a process of "ostensively making common." We conceptualize *understanding* as a state in which two (or more) people experience shared, or aligned, mental representations as a result of communication. As such, understanding can be seen as a first-order outcome of communication. Communication can also result in any number of other outcomes—for example, changing attitudes or behavior; changing the nature of the relationship between people; delineating group boundaries—but we argue that these outcomes are secondary (or tertiary), because they are built on a foundation of understanding, or shared mental representations.

We recognize (and wish to emphasize) that these conceptualizations of "communication" and "understanding" are narrower than that of many contemporary scholars. However, this is necessary for our purposes: when terms are used so liberally that they can refer to anything and everything, it is problematic for theorizing. Narrow definitions allow us to distinguish these constructs from others that are related (e.g. interpretation, meaning-making), and thus to increase the precision of our discussions of—and ultimately, we hope, explanations for—how people create understanding.

Viewing creating understanding as the first-order outcome of communication, we could reframe the question, "How do people create understanding?" to become, "How does the process of communication work?" Superficially, the discipline of communication would seem to have answers to this: nearly every introductory communication textbook features a series of models of communication (e.g. those of Miller & Steinberg, 1975; Schramm, 1954; Shannon & Weaver, 1949; Watzlawick, et al., 1967/2011). However, as the preceding critique of code models illustrates, these models do not provide an accurate depiction of what actually happens when people communicate.

We believe our discipline needs a theoretical framework that addresses understanding as its primary focus, and accurately depicts what happens when people communicate. Specifically, such a framework should both conceptualize understanding, and describe how understanding is created through the process of communicating. Ideally, such a framework should encompass both objective and subjective dimensions of this experience—that is, what happens physically (i.e. in people's brains and bodies, in the material world) and what people consciously experience in the process of creating understanding. Many current models or explanations of communication offer loose or metaphorical descriptions of how communication works (e.g. "sending and receiving messages"); we argue that the discipline needs a framework that offers a physically plausible description of what actually occurs when people communicate, at multiple levels.

A theoretical framework addressing communication as a process of creating understanding should also be able to address the entire range of communicative situations in which people successfully create understanding, including those that involve indirect statements, ambiguous stimuli, or flexible conventions. To do so, this framework needs to move beyond code models and their signal processing perspective on communication, and provide an alternative explanation for how people's communication behavior allows them to achieve states of understanding. As noted in the introduction, there has been considerable theoretical and empirical research conducted outside the discipline of communication that addresses the process of communication, and by extension, understanding. This research and theorizing offer substantial guidance on what a feasible alternative to code models looks like.

To address the level(s) of abstraction and analysis that interest communication researchers, we believe an ostensive-inferential model of communication (Sperber & Wilson, 1995) provides the most viable alternative to a code model. Briefly summarized, an ostensive-inferential model views communication as a process in which communicators make inferences about what each other is thinking or intending based on communicative behavior in context. (We describe this model of communication, including its key claims, in greater detail in subsequent chapters). In this model, inferences about others' thoughts—rather than encoding and decoding using a shared code—are the mechanism through which communication occurs. As such, this model explains how it is possible to communicate successfully when communicators do not share knowledge of a common code, stimuli are ambiguous, or signals are being improvised.

More generally, a theoretical framework addressing communication as a process of creating understanding should also be consistent with theorizing about communication and human psychology from outside the discipline of communication. This includes ideas about the social and cooperative nature of communication and social interaction (e.g. Grice, 1975, 1989; Scott-Phillips, 2015), interactive grounding processes (Clark, 1996; Clark & Brennan, 1991), and conceptualizing successful communication as a form of alignment or entrainment (Hasson et al., 2012; Pickering & Garrod, 2004). It also encompasses current thinking about theory of mind, a capacity required for making inferences about others' thoughts (e.g. Frith & Frith, 2005), mentalizing (e.g. Lieberman, 2013; Scott-Phillips, 2015), and current theorizing about predictive processes in human cognition (e.g. Clark, 2013; Friston & Frith, 2015; Hutchinson & Barrett, 2019).

A theoretical framework addressing the process of creating understanding should also be consistent with the empirical findings from research conducted outside the discipline of communication that addresses these topics directly and indirectly. This includes experimental findings on inference-making (e.g. Wilson & Sperber, 2012), how people engage in grounding (e.g. Clark & Krych, 2004), and how verbal references change across time in interaction (e.g. Holtgraves, 2002). Further, such a theoretical framework should cohere with the recent and growing body of neuroscientific research that provides insight into what happens in people's brains when they communicate and, more generally, when they think about other people (e.g. Hasson et al., 2012; Lieberman, 2013; Stephens et al., 2010).

Finally, we believe the content of a theoretical framework focusing on creating understanding should offer explanations that are consistent with the principles of natural selection and evolutionary theory (e.g. Buss, 1995). Like that of any species, humans' cognition and behavior has evolved over millennia in response to various selection pressures. Thus, any model or framework that seeks to describe or explain human communication should be consistent with theorizing in evolutionary psychology.

In the chapters that follow, we propose a framework that aims to take up this charge. Specifically, the framework we outline conceptualizes communication as a process of social inference-making. Our proposals for mechanisms by which people make inferences are informed by current interdisciplinary research on cognitive science and communication. To date, most models of communication have focused on behavior and mental representations, as people experience them. While these dimensions or levels are certainly important, there is also a neural substrate to them—that is, there is brain activity that corresponds to these forms of physical and mental action. We are not, and do not claim to be, neuroscientists, so brain function is not the focus of our framework or writings. However, to the best of our ability, we aim to propose a framework that is consistent with contemporary neuroscientific research, and to connect our work with findings in this domain. In this, we hope to present a framework that can speak to both the subjective and objective reality of what occurs when we create understanding. In the following chapters, we introduce foundational constructs (Chapter 2), premises (Chapter 3), and key components (Chapter 4) for a process model of creating understanding.

Summary

In this chapter, we have offered a brief summary of the history and current state of the discipline's scholarship on communication and understanding. We have also presented our own perspective on the relationship between these two constructs. We have critiqued the historically dominant approach to conceptualizing communication, code models, and shown that it cannot fully explain human communication. Following from this, we argued that the discipline needs a theoretical framework that explicitly addresses how people create understanding through communication, and outlined what we believe such a framework should include. In the next chapter, we begin to lay the foundation for a theoretical model that focuses on understanding and offers a viable alternative to code models in its depiction of the process of human communication.

References

Angus, I. H., & Lannamann, J. W. (1988). Questioning the institutional boundaries of U.S. communication research: An epistemological inquiry. *Journal of Communication, 38*, 62–74. https://doi.org/10.1111/j.1460-2466.1988.tb02060.x

Bateman, R. M., & Remmers, H. H. (1941). A study of the shifting attitudes of high school students when subjected to favorable and unfavorable propaganda. *Journal of Social Psychology, 13*, 395–406. https://doi.org/10.1080/00224545.1941.9714087

Berger, C. R. (1991). Communication theories and other curios. *Communication Monographs, 58*, 101–113. https://doi.org/10.1080/03637759109376216

Berger, C. R., & Chaffee, S. H. (1987). The study of communication as a science. In C. R. Berger & S. H. Chaffee (Eds.), *Handbook of communication science* (pp. 15–19). SAGE.

Berlo, D. (1960). *The process of communication.* Rinehart & Winston.

Buijzen, M., & Valkenburg, P. M. (2004). Developing a typology of humor in audiovisual media. *Media Psychology, 6*(2), 147–167. https://doi.org/10.1207/s1532785xmep0602_2

Buss, D. M. (1995). Evolutionary psychology: A new paradigm for psychological science. *Psychological Inquiry, 6*, 1–30. https://doi.org/10.1207/s15327965pli0601_1

Clark, A. (2013). Whatever next? Predictive brains, situated agents, and the future of cognitive science. *Behavioral and Brain Sciences, 36*(3), 181–204. https://doi.org/10.1017/S0140525X12000477

Clark, H. H. (1996). *Using language.* Cambridge University Press. https://doi.org/10.1017/CBO9780511620539

Clark, H. H., & Brennan, S. E. (1991). Grounding in communication. In L. B. Resnick, J. M. Levine, & S. D. Teasley (Eds.), *Perspectives on socially shared cognition,* (pp. 127–149). American Psychological Association. https://doi.org/10.1037/10096-006

Clark, H. H., & Krych, M. A. (2004). Speaking while monitoring addressees for understanding. *Journal of Memory and Language, 50*(1), 62–81. https://doi.org/10.1016/j.jml.2003.08.004

Clark, H. H., & Lucy, P. (1975). Understanding what is meant from what is said: A study in conversationally conveyed requests. *Journal of Verbal Learning and Verbal Behavior, 21,* 85–98. https://doi.org/10.1016/S0022-5371(75)80006-5

Coupland, N., Giles, H., & Wiemann, J. M. (1991). *"Miscommunication" and problematic talk.* SAGE.

Delia, J. G. (1987). Communication research: A history. In C. R. Berger & S. H. Chaffee (Eds.), *Handbook of communication science* (pp. 20–98). SAGE.

Desme, A., Mendes, N., Perruche, F., Veillard, E., Elie, C., Moulinet, F., Sanson, F., Georget, J., Tissier, A., Pourriat, J., & Claessens, Y. E. (2013). Nurses' understanding influences comprehension of patients admitted in the observation unit. *Journal of Health Communication, 18*(5), 583–593. https://doi.org/10.1080/10810730.2012.743626

Droba, D. D. (1931). Methods for measuring attitudes. *Psychological Bulletin, 29,* 309–324. https://doi.org/10.1037/h0074726

Festinger, L. (1957). *A theory of cognitive dissonance.* Stanford University Press.

Friston, K. J., & Frith, C. D. (2015). Active inference, communication and hermeneutics. *Cortex, 68,* 129–143. https://doi.org/10.1016/j.cortex.2015.03.025

Frith, C., & Frith, U. (2005). Theory of mind. *Current Biology, 15*(17), R644-R645. https://doi.org/10.1016/j.cub.2005.08.041

Geise, S., & Baden, C. (2014). Putting the image back into the frame: Modeling the linkage between visual communication and frame-processing theory. *Communication Theory, 25*(1), 46–69. https://doi.org/10.1111/comt.12048

Gildea, P., & Glucksberg, S. (1982). On understanding metaphor: The role of context. *Journal of Verbal Learning and Verbal Behavior, 22,* 577–590. https://doi.org/10.1016/S0022-5371(83)90355-9

Grice, H. P. (1975). Logic and conversation. In P. Cole & J. Morgan (Eds.), *Syntax and semantics* (Vol. 3, pp. 41–58). Academic Press.

Grice, H. P. (1989). *Studies in the way of words.* Harvard University Press.

Griffin, E., Ledbetter, A., & Sparks, G. (2019). *A first look at communication theory.* McGraw Hill Education.

Hari, R., & Kujala, M. V. (2009). Brain basis of human social interaction: From concepts to brain imaging. *Physiological Review, 89,* 453–479. https://doi.org/10.1152/physrev.00041.2007

Hasson, U., Ghazanfar, A. A., Galantucci, B., Garrod, S., & Keysers, C. (2012). Brain-to-brain coupling: A mechanism for creating and sharing a social world. *Trends in Cognitive Science, 16*(2), 114–121. https://doi.org/10.1016/j.tics.2011.12.007

Holtgraves, T. M. (2002). *Language as social action: Social psychology and language use.* Lawrence Erlbaum Associates.

Hutchinson, J. B., & Barrett, L. F. (2019). The power of predictions: An emerging paradigm for psychological research. *Current Directions in Psychological Science, 28*(3), 280–291. https://doi.org/10.1177%2F0963721419831992

Knapp, M. L., Vangelisti, A. L., & Caughlin, J. P. (2014). *Interpersonal communication and human relationships* (7th ed.). Allyn & Bacon.

Lang, A. (2000). The limited capacity model of mediated message processing. *Journal of Communication, 50*(1), 46–70. https://doi.org/10.1111/j.1460-2466.2000.tb02833.x

Lang, A. (2017). Limited capacity model of motivated mediated message processing (LC4MP). In P. Rossler, C. A. Hefner & L. van Zoonen (Eds.), *The international encyclopedia of media effects* (pp. 851–860). Wiley-Blackwell. https://doi.org/10.1002/9781118783764.wbieme0077

Lazersfeld, P. F., & Stanton, F. N. (1949). *Communications research, 1948-1949.* Harper & Row.

Lieberman, M. D. (2013). *Social: Why our brains are wired to connect.* Broadway Books.

Lippman, W. (1922). *Public opinion.* MacMillan.

Majerovitz, S. D., Greene, M. G., Adelman, R. D., Brody, G. M., Leber, K., & Healy, S. W. (1997). Older patients' understanding of medical information in the emergency department. *Health Communication, 9*(3), 237–251. https://doi.org/10.1207/s15327027hc0903_3

Mazor, K. M., Calvi, J., Cowan, R., Costanza, M. E., Han, P. K., Greene, S. M., Saccoccio, L., Cove, E., Roblin, D., & Williams, A. (2010). Media messages about cancer: what do people understand? *Journal of Health Communication, 15*(S2), 126–145. https://doi.org/10.1080/10810730.2010 499983

Mead, G. H. (1934). *Mind, self, and society.* University of Chicago Press.

Miller, G. R., & Steinberg, M. (1975). *Between people: A new analysis of interpersonal communication.* Science Research Associates.

Misyak, J., Noguchi, T., & Chater, N. (2016). Instantaneous conventions: The emergence of flexible communicative signals. *Psychological Science, 27*(12), 1550–1561. https://doi.org/10.1177/0956797616661199

Murphy, G., Murphy, L. B., & Newcomb, T. M. (1937). *Experimental social psychology.* Harper & Row.

Nafziger, R. O. (1937). World war correspondents and the censorship of the belligerents. *Public Opinion Quarterly, 14*, 226–243. https://doi.org/10.1177/107769903701400302

Osborn, W. W. (1939). An experiment in teaching resistance to propaganda. *Journal of Experimental Education, 8*, 1–17. https://doi.org/10.1080/00220973.1939.11010142

Park, R. E. (1940). News as a form of knowledge: A chapter in the sociology of knowledge. *Journal of Sociology, 45*, 669–686. https://doi.org/10.1086/218445

Pickering, M. J., & Garrod, S. (2004). Toward a mechanistic psychology of dialogue. *Behavioral and Brain Sciences, 27*(2), 169–190. https://doi.org/10.1017/S0140525X04000056

Pickering, M. J., & Garrod, S. (2006). Alignment as the basis for successful communication. *Research on Language and Computation, 4*(2–3), 203–228. https://doi.org/10.1007/s11168-006-9004-0

Rains, S., Keating, D., Banas, J., Richards, A., & Palomares, N. (2020, May). *The state and evolution of communication research from 1918-2015.* Paper presented at the 70th International Communication Association Annual Conference, Virtual Meeting.

Schramm, W. (1954). How communication works. In W. Schramm (Ed.), *The processes and effects of mass communication* (pp. 3–26). University of Illinois Press.

Scott-Phillips, T. C. (2015). *Speaking our minds: Why human communication is different, and how language evolved to make it special.* Palgrave Macmillan.

Shannon, C. E., & Weaver, W. (1949). *The mathematical theory of communication.* University of Illinois Press.

Sillars, A. L. (1998). (Mis)Understanding. In B. H. Spitzberg & W. R. Cupach (Eds.), *The dark side of personal relationships* (pp. 73–102). Erlbaum.

Sillars, A., Koerner, A., & Fitzpatrick, M. A. (2005). Communication and understanding in parent–adolescent relationships. *Human Communication Research, 31*(1), 102–128. https://doi.org/10.1111/j.1468-2958.2005.tb00866.x

Sperber, D., & Wilson, D. (1995). *Relevance: Communication and cognition (2nd Ed.).* Oxford, UK: Blackwell.

Stephens, G. J., Silbert, L. J., & Hasson, U. (2010). Speaker-listener neural coupling underlies successful communication. *Proceedings of the National Academy of Sciences, 107,* 14425–14430. https://doi.org/10.1073/pnas.1008662107

Stone, E. R., Gabard, A. R., Groves, A. E., & Lipkus, I. M. (2015). Effects of numerical versus foreground-only icon displays on understanding of risk magnitudes. *Journal of Health Communication, 20*(10), 1230–1241. https://doi.org/10.1080/10810730.2015.1018594

Thompson, D. & Filik, R. (2016). Sarcasm in written communication: Emoticons are efficient markers of intention, *Journal of Computer-Mediated Communication, 21*(2), 105–120. https://doi.org/10.1111/jcc4.12156

Watzlawick, P., Bavelas, J. B., & Jackson, D. D. (1967/2011). *Pragmatics of human communication: A study of interactional patterns, pathologies and paradoxes.* W.W. Norton & Company.

West, R., & Turner, L. H. (2018). *Introducing communication theory: Analysis and application.* McGraw-Hill Education.

Wiemann, J. M., Hawkins, R. P., & Pingree, S. (1988). Fragmentation in the field—and the movement toward integration in communication science. *Human Communication Research, 15,* 304–310. https://doi.org/10.1111/j.1468-2958.1988.tb00186.x.

Wilson, D., & Sperber, D. (2012). *Meaning and relevance.* Cambridge University Press. https://doi.org/10.1017/CBO9781139028370

CHAPTER TWO

Conceptualizing Understanding

In this chapter, we introduce foundational constructs for studying understanding, including social stimuli *(i.e. sensory input that produces a cognitive, affective, or behavioral reaction),* meme states *(i.e. mental representations of concepts, ideas, or experiences) and* situation models *(i.e. multifaceted mental representations of a communicative episode). We then use these concepts to articulate our conceptualization of* understanding *as two (or more) people experiencing entrainment of their situation models.*

In this chapter, we focus on the constructs that serve as a foundation for modeling how people create understanding. In this, we also introduce the associated terminology—some of which will likely be new to readers—that we will use to discuss understanding, and how people create understanding in interaction.

Before proceeding, we would like to offer a brief remark about terminology and language use in this book. One of the biggest challenges we have had discussing understanding—between ourselves as colleagues and co-authors; with our students in classes; and in writing this book—has been that of language. The vocabulary that communication scholars have to discuss communication is an indirect product of decades of theorizing (or in some cases, lack of theorizing) about this topic. In many cases, this means that current ways of talking about communication implicitly reinforce a code model or signal processing perspective. For instance, terms like "sender" and "receiver", and describing communication as a process of "sending messages", are ubiquitous, and difficult to work around. However, these terms have problematic implications: they suggest that people play distinct and independent roles in the process of communicating, and that ideas are somehow packaged and transported from one place to another when people communicate.

This vocabulary is not well-suited for the way that we wish to conceptualize communication and understanding (e.g. as intrinsically dyadic endeavors). In the chapters that follow, we have done our best to avoid these traditional ways of describing communicative phenomena because we do not wish to implicitly reinforce a monologic, code model perspective. When we do invoke more traditional terminology, we primarily do so in order to draw and clarify connections to existing scholarship. In these cases, we use our preferred terminology in the main text of a sentence, followed by the traditional term in parentheses. We also follow this convention when summarizing theories from other areas that use similar concepts our own, but label them differently. Like all scholars, we are standing on the shoulders of giants, and we want to acknowledge the intellectual debt we owe to those who have come before us. However, we are also aware of the power of language to implicitly reinforce and reify perspectives (e.g. Beukeboom, 2013; Sutton, 2010), and have made choices about our language use accordingly.

Foundational Terms and Assumptions

Distinguishing Stimuli and Memes

We now turn our attention to introducing key concepts and related assumptions that serve as a starting point for conceptualizing understanding. To begin, we define the basic components of communication as a process. As outlined in Chapter 1, we conceptualize communication as a process in which people share, or make common, their thoughts. However, concepts or ideas do not have any material form, and as such cannot (physically) travel across time and space (e.g. Shannon & Weaver, 1949). In classic "code models" of communication, this issue is addressed through the use of *codes* and *signals*. Concepts or ideas are encoded into physical signals that travel across time and space; these signals are subsequently decoded back into concepts or ideas at their destination (Shannon & Weaver, 1949). As discussed in the previous chapter, this view of communication is not wholly inaccurate, but it has considerable limitations, and does not adequately describe or explain much of everyday human communication.

As a basis for a broader, more comprehensive description of human communication (following Sperber & Wilson, 1995, among others), we propose it is more useful to describe the process of communication—and thus explain how concepts or ideas "travel"—in terms of *stimuli* and *memes* (or *meme states*). We define *stimuli* as any kind of sensory input (i.e. something in people's environment that is accessible to them via hearing, sight, touch, taste, or smell) that produces a cognitive, affective, or behavioral reaction. Any environment people are in contains energy in many different forms (e.g. various frequencies of sound, light with various wavelengths). However, people cannot perceive all of it: human senses can only sample from a narrow set of non-overlapping bandwidths of that energy. In any given instance, we only attend to some portions of those bandwidths, while other portions of those bandwidths are processed at very low levels of awareness, or not processed at all. We use *stimuli* to refer to the portions of those bandwidths that (a) are accessible to our senses, and (b) evoke, or bring about, some kind of response, as opposed to just being present in an environment. Stimuli have a physical or material form, and are directly accessible to multiple people.

Stimuli can manifest in many ways: a stimulus could be the sound of a voice, the smell of someone's perfume, a gesture, markings on a page, a facial movement or expression, or the act of taking someone's hand, among many other things. Most of the stimuli we will focus on in our discussions of creating understanding are *social* to varying degrees. We consider stimuli to be *social stimuli* to the extent that they come from and are intended for other people, or are used for purposes that relate to other people.

Memes, in turn, are people's mental renderings of concepts, ideas, and experiences. Memes exist in the mind of an individual and are not directly accessible to other people. Drawing on Dawkins' (1976) use of the term *meme* as a bounded unit of cultural transmission, we conceptualize memes as discrete mental units that are capable of being shared and modified via social interaction (see also Dennett, 2017). Dawkins (1976) thought of a meme as comparable to a gene. Genes are replicators whose likelihood of being replicated was directly tied to the value it had for the host. Dawkins thought certain ideas—memes—would be more likely to be replicated, shared, or communicated if they proved valuable to the communicators that "host" them. (The word "meme" is modeled on "gene", using the Greek word "mimēa", meaning "that which is imitated"). These properties of memes offer useful dimensions for thinking about the content of our minds in ways not shared by related terms such as *concepts, thoughts, cognitions,* and *ideas*. Conceptualizing the contents of our minds as memes highlights features like cultural transmission, host value, and replicability.

As we conceptualize them, memes can vary in their complexity. When people think of a single object (e.g. a dog) or concept (e.g. love), the corresponding meme is relatively simple and straightforward. However, memes can also be considerably more complicated, involving multiple lower-level memes and specified relationships between them. Just as the human body is a unit that comprises many individual sub-units (e.g. limbs, organs), which are in turn comprised of smaller units (e.g. cells), more complex memes can be comprised of multiple elements, each of which could be considered a meme on its own. However, at a given level of abstraction, a meme is a bounded unit that can be represented and labeled as such.

Stimuli and *memes* are conceptually distinct, and this distinction is well-established. Ancient Greek philosophers differentiated these two concepts in their discussions of the nature of signs, and the *signed* and *signifier*[1] are foundational concepts, distinguished from one another, in the study of semiotics (e.g. de Saussure, 1911/2004). Similarly, a cursory comparison of any two languages or dialects clearly demonstrates that different *stimuli* (in this case, words) can be used to call to mind the same *meme state* (i.e. concept), indicating these two are distinct (Zinszer et al., 2016). Although few contemporary communication researchers would dispute this distinction, it is often glossed over in the way communicative processes are described. "Message", in particular, is a term that is used widely but ambiguously in communication scholarship: while some researchers use the term to indicate a physical manifestation or set of objective features (*stimuli*), others use it to refer to the mental representation or experience evoked (*meme*) (e.g. O'Keefe, 2003). We believe that making a clear distinction between these concepts, and using terminology that consistently reflects this distinction, is important for describing and explaining the process of creating understanding in a precise manner.

Thus, stated formally, one assumption of our framework is that *memes* (mental representations) are distinct from *stimuli* (manifest, material expressions), and they have different properties: memes are internal and accessible only to a given individual via his or her mind; stimuli are external and are accessible to multiple individuals via their senses.

Activating Meme States

Having made this distinction, we now turn to the how stimuli and memes relate to each other. A second assumption of our framework is that when people perceive and attend to stimuli, those stimuli *activate* particular memes in context (e.g. Pickering & Garrod, 2006, p. 221). This notion is grounded in models of human cognition and memory, which tell us that we can access memes stored in our memory when we are prompted to by some kind of cue, or stimulus, that is associated with that meme (Henke, 2010; Rudmann, 2018). When we do encounter such a stimulus, the associated meme is brought to mind: the meme is *activated*.

Generally, memes that have been recently activated are easier to activate in the present and (near) future (Pickering & Garrod, 2004; 2006); that is, they have a higher *resting level of activation* (Sharwood Smith, 2019).

According to most widely accepted models of human memory and cognition, memes do not exist in isolation; rather, they are connected to one another (e.g. Collins & Loftus, 1975). These connections are created when something is initially learned, or encoded into memory, which involves physiological changes in the brain (referred to as *memory traces*). Connections may also be made in the processes of recall and active reflection on items in memory. The number and nature of connections between memes can and do vary from meme to meme (potentially, although not exclusively, as a function of the type of processing involved; for a model of memory organized by processing modes, see Henke, 2010). An important consequence of associations between memes is that activating one meme can affect or activate other memes that are connected to it. More specifically, activation of one meme can lead to spreading activation across other, related memes (e.g. Collins & Loftus, 1975; Pickering & Garrod, 2004; Scherer & Wentura, 2018).

We now return to our earlier assertion that when people perceive and attend to stimuli, those stimuli activate memes (more specifically, meme states; see below) in context. We use the term *activate* to highlight the rapid and often unconscious nature of how stimuli bring a meme to people's conscious awareness, or working memory. In most cases, attending to a sound, image, smell, taste, or texture immediately brings to mind some form of mental representation. People generally do not have to try or extend any conscious effort to have these mental experiences; they are so immediate that people may not distinguish them from "objective" reality. (This point has been the object of much discussion in scholarship on perception as well as philosophy of science; see for example, Hanson's [1969/2002] discussion of *seeing* versus *seeing as*). In practical terms, the process of rapid meme activation means that people experience the world in terms of objects, actions, and intentions brought to mind by stimuli, rather than in terms of the actual stimuli. For example, people subjectively experience (i.e. "see", "hear") *a person laughing* rather than a series of changes in color and lines in their visual field and compressions and rarefications of air hitting their eardrums.

In practice, memes are always activated in context (e.g. having a conversation, reading a text, listening to a speech or piece of music, etc.). As we discuss further in Chapter 4, the context in which the meme is activated provides stimuli (that may or may not be social in nature) that also activate memes. As just described, activation of a given meme in context results in a spreading activation pattern across other memes that are associated with the focal meme. Thus, when people encounter a stimulus in context, it activates more than a single meme; it activates a complex of memes that are associated through previous experience, and influenced by current context. We refer to this complex as a *meme state*. For example, we can talk about the meme "dog" in the abstract, but the visual stimuli "d-o-g" or the corresponding oral utterance of "dog" will activate a meme state that reflects—to varying degrees—other memes that have become associated with the meme "dog", as well as memes associated with the present context in which the utterance takes place. The "dog" meme state that is activated via the utterance, "That dog is good with kids" may thus be different than the "dog" meme state activated via the utterance, "That dog is the one that bit me." The meme states activated through interaction are dynamic; as new stimuli are presented and perceived, the meme states that are activated are updated and changed.

Situation Models

As part of the process of communicating, people also construct higher-order mental representations of communicative episodes: these are *situation models*. A situation model is a "multi-dimensional representation of the situation under discussion" (Pickering & Garrod, 2004, p. 172; see also Kintsch & van Dijk, 1978). Essentially, situation models capture the content and nature of a communicative episode at a given point in time. Described in our terminology, situation models consist of activated meme states and their structural relationships to each other. They also include pragmatic and functional information related to a communicative episode (such as whether an utterance is a statement or a request; e.g. Searle, 1969). For instance, a situation model could represent an interaction as "greeting colleagues", "exchanging observations about changes in daily life during a pandemic", or "seeking social support for the loss of a loved one." In each case, the corresponding situation model would include meme states addressing the people involved and various components of the content being addressed (e.g. the nature of the greeting; the content of observations; the nature of the problem and type of support being sought or provided). The situation model would also include the relationships or connections between those components (e.g. in the final example, how the components of the problem relate to each other and comprise a larger whole, how the problem causes the need for a particular type of support, and how the support provided attempts to meet that need).

We conceptualize situation models as both descriptive and predictive: to the extent that they model what is happening in a given communicative situation, they can be used to generate informed hypotheses about what will occur next. As we conceptualize it, the function of a situation model is to accurately reflect the state and nature of the communicative episode (Friston, 2010). Because communication is a joint endeavor, this includes accurately representing what other interactants are thinking and doing. Situation models are dynamic; as new meme states are activated (through communicators' presentation of stimuli), communicators' situation models are updated and change accordingly. (A more detailed discussion of this proposed process is provided in Chapter 4 and Chapter 5). Like meme states, situation models are internal and accessible only to their owner.

In sum, both meme states and situation models are internal mental renderings of concepts, ideas and experiences that are accessible only to their owners. As such they cannot be shared directly. However, stimuli have a physical form and are accessible to multiple individuals, and can activate memes states, and consequently contribute to situation models. Thus, when people want to share a meme state and/or situation model with another person, they use (i.e. select, present, attend to, and interpret) stimuli as a means to accomplish this goal. This, we argue, is the essence of what happens when people communicate with the goal of creating understanding: communicators use stimuli to activate meme states in their interlocutors' minds. This, in turn, drives the construction, development, and refinement of their interlocutors' situation models (see Chapter 5).

Conceptualizing Understanding

Having articulated and established that stimuli and memes are distinct, and that attending to stimuli activates meme states, we can now offer a working definition of *understanding,* the central focus of this book. Specifically, we conceptualize *understanding* as *two (or more) people experiencing entrainment of situation models as a result of at least one person's use of social stimuli.* In this definition, *entrainment* refers to experiencing congruent situation models, and related meme states (i.e. mental representations).

For two situation models to be congruent, they must share essential features or qualities relevant to the current context, but they need not be identical in all respects or dimensions. The degree and nature of these shared features or qualities depends on the demands of the task at hand, as well as communicators' desires (see below). In face-to-face interaction, entrainment of situation models is typically coordinated in time and across time. In other communicative contexts (e.g. reading a book), people's experiences of congruent situation models may occur at different points in time. However, we generally expect them to be temporally coordinated relative to the content of the communication. For example, following our conceptualization, someone reading page 120 of a book would experience a situation model that is congruent with the situation model the author had when writing the text on page 120.

Generally, we consider communicators to have successfully created understanding when their situation models are sufficiently congruent and coordinated for their present purposes. These purposes can and will vary from situation to situation, such that different degrees of entrainment may be required for understanding in different contexts. In some cases, such as discussing plans for a rocket launch, a high degree of precision is required. In these situations, we would expect communicators' situation models (and their component meme states) to be highly congruent and tightly entrained, down to the smallest detail.

In other cases, communicators may wish to be strategically ambiguous, or may not have an unambiguous or fully formed meme state to communicate. For instance, if two people are discussing how they feel about unfolding current events, and they are still forming opinions about those events, neither individual may have a well-defined mental representation of their opinions. In these situations, we would not expect two peoples' situation models (and component meme states) to be highly similar or entrained in their details. However, we would expect them to be similar or entrained in broad strokes, at a higher level of abstraction, if some degree of understanding has been successfully created. (Indeed, their entrained situation models might include their uncertainty about their own, and each other's, opinions). Similarly, if two people are talking about "dogs" generically, it may be fine for one to mentally represent a prototypical "dog" as a Golden Retriever, and the other as an Australian Shephard. However, if two people are talking about a specific dog—for example, "Sally's dog"—then their mental representations must match at a higher level of detail and precision for understanding to occur.

In short, when people understand each other, their mental representations of an experience, event, or concept converge in a given moment; if understanding is sustained, these mental representations are coordinated across time. This entrainment, or convergence and coordination of situation models, is a transitory state that communicators move in and out of across, and through, interaction. When communicators realize they are no longer entraining, this can be an impetus to initiate repair strategies, a topic that we will address in greater detail in Chapter 6 (see also Pickering & Garrod, 2004, 2006). To the extent that communicators ultimately experience functionally similar, or aligned, situation models as an interaction progresses, we can describe them as successfully creating understanding. Thus, creating understanding results in entraining and aligning mental representations between people, or coordinating minds so they are—in lay terms—thinking the same thing (Pickering & Garrod, 2004, 2006, 2013).

The conceptualization of understanding as a form of entrainment or alignment of mental content draws on both theory and empirical research related to this topic across disciplines. Sperber and Wilson (1995) describe the process of ostensive-inferential communication as "a process involving two information-processing devices. One device modifies the physical environment of the other. As a result, the *second device constructs representations similar to representations already stored in the first device*" (p. 1; our italics). Similarly, Pickering and Garrod's (2004, 2006) *interactive alignment model* describes successful communication as a process in which interactants' situation models become aligned. As we view communication as a process in which the fundamental goal is creating understanding (see Chapter 1), the definition we propose is consistent with this work (even if these scholars do not explicitly reference "understanding").

The definition we propose is also broadly consistent with Clark and colleagues' work on *grounding*, which describes how people construct and manage shared mental representations in interaction (e.g. Clark, 1996; Clark & Brennan, 1991). Research on grounding typically focuses on participants' use of stimuli to negotiate *common ground* (defined as mutual or shared beliefs, assumptions, and knowledge). Clark and colleagues have argued that people generally assume that they have successfully established common ground in interaction unless they encounter evidence to the contrary. Scholarship on common ground and grounding generally emphasizes how people arrive at *beliefs* about understanding, rather than understanding itself. However, Clark and colleagues' treatment of communication as a process of negotiating shared or common mental representations coheres with our conceptualizations of both communication and understanding.

Our conceptualization of understanding is also consistent with the conceptual and operational definitions used by Sillars and colleagues in their empirical work on cognition in communication. Specifically, these researchers studied cognition during conflict in married couples (Sillars et al., 2000) and communication between parents and adolescents (Sillars et al., 2005). In these studies, interactions between participants were recorded, and then a video-assisted recall procedure was used to ask each participant what they were thinking, and what they thought their partner was thinking, at regular intervals during the recorded interaction. In these studies, understanding is conceptualized and operationalized as individuals (i.e. each member of a couple, or a parent and adolescent) having aligned responses at approximately the same time in an interaction.

Finally, the conceptualization of understanding as experiencing congruent, or functionally similar, mental states is also consistent with recent neuroscientific research on communication. This work has demonstrated that when people communicate successfully—that is, when they understand each other—patterns of neural activation become synchronized, or entrained, across brains (Hasson et al., 2012; Leong et al., 2017; Nguyen et al., 2019; Stephens et al., 2010). In other words, people's brains enter into transient states of coupled neural activity when people communicate successfully. Thus, conceptualizing understanding as entraining situation models is not just a description of subjectively accessible mental experiences; it also has a physical and physiological basis.

Summary

In this chapter, we have introduced foundational assumptions, terms, and definitions for studying understanding. We distinguished between stimuli (sensory input that produces a cognitive, affective, or behavioral reaction), meme states (mental representations of concepts, ideas, or experiences) and situation models (higher order, multifaceted mental representations of a communicative episode). We then explained that stimuli activate meme states for communicators in interaction, and that this activation contributes to the development and refinement of communicators' situation models. We also provided an explicit conceptualization of understanding as *two (or more) people experiencing entrainment of their situation models as a result of at least one person's use of social stimuli*. This conceptualization is consistent with theoretical and empirical work in cognitive science, psychology, communication, and neuroscience. Defining understanding as process of entrainment achieved between two (or more) people also positions understanding as minimally dyadic, or joint, in nature. Having defined understanding, the next question becomes: How do people accomplish this in interaction? In the following chapters, we work toward addressing this question.

Note

1. Here, we wish to briefly note that we have consciously chosen not to use terms involving variants of "sign" or "symbol" in this text. Typical definitions and usage of these terms rely on the idea that one thing is "standing for" another, which connotes fixed and specific relationships between stimuli and meme states. In our view, this adheres too closely to a code model perspective on communication, and does not allow for sufficient flexibility to capture what occurs in a wide range of different communicative situations.

References

Beukeboom, C. (2013). Mechanisms of language bias. In J. Forgas, J. László, & V. Orsolya (Eds.), *Social cognition and communication* (pp. 313–330). Psychology Press.

Clark, H. H. (1996). *Using language*. Cambridge University Press. https://doi.org/10.1017/CBO9780511620539

Clark, H. H., & Brennan, S. E. (1991). Grounding in communication. In L. B. Resnick, J. M. Levine, & S. D. Teasley (Eds.), *Perspectives on socially shared cognition*, (pp. 127–149). American Psychological Association. https://doi.org/10.1037/10096-006

Collins, A. M., & Loftus, E. F. (1975). A spreading-activation theory of semantic processing. *Psychological Review, 82*(6), 407–428. https://doi.org/10.1037/0033-295X.82.6.407

Dawkins, R. (1976). *The selfish gene*. Oxford University Press.

Dennett, D. C. (2017). *From bacteria to Bach and back: The evolution of minds*. W. W. Norton & Company.

de Saussure, F. (1911/2004). Course in general linguistics. In J. Rivkin and M. Ryan (Eds.), *Literary theory: An anthology, 2nd edition* (pp. 59–71). Blackwell.

Friston, K. (2010). The free-energy principle: A unified brain theory? *Nature Reviews Neuroscience, 11*(2), 127–138. https://doi.org/10.1038/nrn2787

Hanson, R. N. (1969/2002). Perception and discovery. In Y. Balashov & A. Rosenberg (Eds.), *Philosophy of science: Contemporary readings* (pp. 321–349). Routledge.

Hasson, U., Ghazanfar, A. A., Galantucci, B., Garrod, S., & Keysers, C. (2012). Brain-to-brain coupling: A mechanism for creating and sharing a social world. *Trends in Cognitive Science, 16*(2), 114–121. https://doi.org/10.1016/j.tics.2011.12.007

Henke, K. (2010). A model for memory systems based on processing modes rather than consciousness. *Nature Reviews Neuroscience, 11*(7), 523–532. https://doi.org/10.1038/nrn2850

Kintsch, W., & Van Dijk, T. A. (1978). Toward a model of text comprehension and production. *Psychological Review, 85*(5), 363–394. https://doi.org/10.1037/0033-295X.85.5.363

Leong, V., Byrne, E., Clackson, K., Georgieva, S., Lam, S., & Wass, S. (2017). Speaker gaze increases information coupling between infant and adult brains. *Proceedings of the National Academy of Sciences, 114*(50), 13290–13295. https://doi.org/10.1073/pnas.1702493114

Nguyen, M., Vanderwal, T., & Hasson, U. (2019). Shared understanding of narratives is correlated with shared neural responses. *NeuroImage, 184*(1), 161–170. https://doi.org/10.1016/j.neuroimage.2018.09.010

O'Keefe, D. J. (2003). Message properties, mediating states, and manipulation checks: Claims, evidence, and data analysis in experimental persuasive message effects research. *Communication Theory, 13*(3), 251–274. https://doi.org/10.1111/j.1468-2885.2003.tb00292.x

Pickering, M. J., & Garrod, S. (2004). Toward a mechanistic psychology of dialogue. *Behavioral and Brain Sciences, 27*(2), 169–190 https://doi.org/10.1017/S0140525X04000056

Pickering, M. J., & Garrod, S. (2006). Alignment as the basis for successful communication. *Research on Language and Computation, 4*(2–3), 203–228. https://doi.org/10.1007/s11168-006-9004-0

Pickering, M. J., & Garrod, S. (2013). An integrated theory of language production and comprehension. *Behavioral and Brain Sciences, 36*(4), 329–347. https://doi.org/10.1017/S0140525X12001495

Rudmann, D. (2018). *Learning and memory.* SAGE.

Scherer, D., & Wentura, D. (2018). Combining the post-cue task and the perceptual identification task to assess parallel activation and mutual facilitation of related primes and targets. *Experimental Psychology 65*(2), 84–97. https://doi.org/10.1027/1618-3169/a000396

Searle, J. R. (1969). *Speech acts: An essay in the philosophy of language.* Cambridge University Press. https://doi.org/10.1017/CBO9781139173438

Shannon, C. E., & Weaver, W. (1949). *The mathematical theory of communication.* University of Illinois Press.

Sharwood Smith, M. (2019). The compatibility within a modular framework of emergent and dynamical processes in mind and brain. *Journal of Neurolinguistics, 49*, 240–244. https://doi.org/10.1016/j.jneuroling.2018.04.010

Sillars, A., Koerner, A., & Fitzpatrick, M. A. (2005). Communication and understanding in parent–adolescent relationships. *Human Communication Research, 31*(1), 102–128. https://doi.org/10.1111/j.1468-2958.2005.tb00866.x

Sillars, A., Roberts, L. J., Leonard, K. E., & Dun, T. (2000). Cognition during marital conflict: The relationship of thought and talk. *Journal of Social and Personal Relationships, 17*(4–5), 479–502. https://doi.org/10.1177/0265407500174002

Sperber, D., & Wilson, D. (1995). *Relevance: Communication and cognition (2nd Ed.).* Blackwell.

Stephens, G. J., Silbert, L. J., & Hasson, U. (2010). Speaker-listener neural coupling underlies successful communication. *Proceedings of the National Academy of Sciences, 107*, 14425–14430. https://doi.org/10.1073/pnas.1008662107

Sutton, R. M. (2010). The creative power in language in social cognition and intergroup relations. In H. Giles, S. Reid, & J. Harwood (Eds.), *The dynamics of intergroup communication* (pp. 105–116). Peter Lang.

Zinszer, B. D., Anderson, A. J., Kang, O., Wheatley, T., & Raizada, R. D. (2016). Semantic structural alignment of neural representational spaces enables translation between English and Chinese words. *Journal of Cognitive Neuroscience, 28*(11), 1749–1759. https://doi.org/10.1162/jocn_a_01000

CHAPTER THREE

Premises: Human Cognition and Behavior

In this chapter, we present three interrelated observations about human cognition and behavior that serve as premises for explaining how people create understanding. Specifically, we observe that human beings are fundamentally social in orientation; that human mental processes are governed by a predisposition for efficiency; and that predictive inference-making is a core feature of human mental activity. We review and synthesize evidence for each of these observations, and discuss their potential evolutionary basis.

Having defined *understanding* as a state in which two (or more) people experience entrainment of their situation models as a result of at least one person's use of social stimuli, we now turn our attention to addressing how people achieve this outcome—that is, how people create understanding in social interaction. The best answers to "how" questions are typically models of a process, and this is what we will ultimately propose: a process model of creating understanding. However, before proposing such a model, we wish to lay a firm foundation. The concepts of *stimuli, meme states,* and *situation models* constitute a start. In this chapter, we finish the foundation by presenting a set of premises for our model.

More specifically, we present a set of interrelated observations about the nature of humans' brains and behavior that hold across contexts, and serve as premises for our model of creating understanding. We contend that these observations govern, and by extension can explain, much of human interaction, and therefore how people create understanding. We also contend that the content of these observations is the product of natural selection—that is, they are adaptations that have helped improve humans' likelihood of survival, from an evolutionary perspective. In what follows, we present these interrelated observations, reviewing evidence for each, and outlining how the qualities they describe potentially offer adaptive advantages.

Premise 1: Social Orientation

Our first observation is that humans have a fundamental social orientation. People are, at the most basic level, social animals: they are innately motivated to use their mental energy and capacities in ways that relate to other people (i.e. their conspecifics) (e.g. Lieberman, 2013). This is not a novel observation; indeed, versions of it constitute the basis for various disciplines and subdisciplines of academic inquiry, such as sociology and social psychology. However, we believe it is important to underscore, given its central role in understanding.

Evidence

There are several lines of evidence that support a fundamental social orientation in human cognition (though we emphasize that what we summarize here is far from an exhaustive inventory). These lines of evidence encompass both people's subjective psychological experiences and the brain activity that underlies these experiences. First and perhaps foremost is the human capacity for *theory of mind*. Theory of mind is the ability to recognize that other people have minds, and by extension thoughts, intentions, and motives—and that these mental experiences guide other people's behavior (Frith & Frith, 2005). Embedded in the concept of theory of mind is also the recognition that others' thoughts and mental experiences may not be the same as one's own—that is, that others can perceive, think, and feel differently than oneself does. For example, other people can have false beliefs, dissimilar opinions, or different interpretations of events.

Closely related is people's capacity, and propensity, to think about what other people are thinking. Inferring what others are thinking has been termed *mindreading* (e.g. Apperly, 2018; Scott-Phillips, 2015) or *mentalizing* (Frith & Frith, 2006, 2012; Heyes, 2014; Lieberman, 2013); we address this topic in more detail below. At least some forms of mentalizing, such as visual perspective-taking, appear to occur spontaneously (Apperly, 2018), suggesting mentalizing is an innate human tendency. Indeed, in social interactions, people typically do not "see" or interpret social stimuli objectively. Rather, they generally perceive and think about other entities in terms of mental states; that is, they tend to interpret other entities' actions as behaviors of agents with intentions (e.g. Dennett, 1987, 2017; Rossett, 2008). Thus, neurotypical people see a person waving his or her hand not as "a moving hand attached to a body", but as "a person [agent] greeting me [intention]" or "a person [agent] trying to get my attention [intention]."

The human tendency to experience the world in terms of mental states, agents, and intentions is so pervasive that people readily overgeneralize (Dennett, 2017). For instance, people frequently extend mental state attributions to inanimate objects. A well-known illustration of this is a study by social psychologists Heider and Simmel (1944), in which participants watched a short (less than 90 second) animated film of two triangles and a circle moving in and around a rectangle. When asked what they had seen, participants described the film's shapes in animate, agentic terms—that is, they attributed social agency (including goals and emotions) to the triangles and circle, despite rationally knowing that they were shapes on a screen that did not have thoughts or feelings.[1]

The tendency to overgeneralize mental state explanations can also be seen in comments in which people anthropomorphize everyday objects like cars or appliances (e.g. "My computer is mad at me"). Rationally, people know that their computer does not (yet) have emotional experiences that affect its performance. However, the interpretation of the situation that is most accessible, reflected in the language that most readily comes to people, is often framed in terms of agents, intentions, and mental states.

A separate but conceptually related phenomenon that provides additional evidence for a people's social orientation is the prevalence of *face pareidolia*. This term describes people's tendency to see faces in non-social stimuli such as the headlights and grill configuration in the front of cars. There are also many instances of people claiming to "see" the face of religious figures such as Jesus in various objects (e.g. stains on fabric; burn patterns on toast) (Kato & Mugitani, 2015; Liu et al., 2014). Perceiving faces in this way suggests that people are, on a basic level, inclined to anticipate (and seek) visual indications of the presence of other people.

People's social orientation in cognition can also be seen indirectly through their communicative behavior. Dunbar (2004) has observed that approximately two thirds of casual conversation is devoted to social topics, or "gossip." Additionally, when people (especially children) lack motivation or desire to engage in social interaction, it is seen as developmentally problematic (e.g. Baron-Cohen, 1997). In some cases, a lack of desire for social engagement may be classified as a psychological disorder (e.g. Chevallier et al., 2012). Both the presence of a societal expectation that a desire for social interaction is normative and people's apparent desire to use social situations to discuss social topics are good evidence that people have a drive for social engagement.

A strong desire for social interaction is also visible in everyday human behavior. People consistently seek out social engagement and social relationships across all domains of their lives (e.g. friendships, romantic relationships, professional ties), and seek the support of other people in times of need (e.g. social support). Research across a range of disciplines provides ample evidence for positive psychological and physical effects of social connection, and detrimental psychological and physical effects of social isolation (e.g. Cacioppo & Cacioppo, 2014; Cohen, 2004; Holt-Lunstad et al., 2010; Umberson et al., 2010; Yang et al., 2015).

There is also a growing body of evidence supporting a fundamental social orientation in humans' brain activity and architecture. One example is the presence of dedicated and/or focused brain systems for social thinking. Neuroscientific research suggests that people recruit different brain regions to solve social problems than to solve non-social problems or engage in deductive reasoning (Lieberman, 2013). Closely related, experimental studies have found that people appear to process false belief information (i.e. content framed as another's person's thoughts) differently, and more rapidly, than analogous, non-social representations of false information (i.e. the same content presented as a visual image or in a written note) (Cohen & German, 2010; Cohen et al., 2015).

Recent findings regarding the brain's *default mode network* activity provide additional evidence for the primacy of social thinking in the brain function. The default mode network is a network of cortical activity that is engaged when the brain is "at rest"—in other words, when people are not asked to focus on anything or engage in a specific mental task (e.g. Binder et al., 1999; Greicius et al., 2003). Spunt et al. (2015) found that activity exhibited in part of the default mode network (in particular, the dorsomedial prefrontal cortex) was similar to the activity that is visible when people think about other people's mental states. The researchers also found that the stronger participants' default mode network activation in this area was, the more efficient they were at responding to questions involving other people's mental states in a subsequent task. Levels of default mode network activity were also positively correlated with participants' self-reported social skills. The researchers interpreted these findings as indicating that the brain's default, resting state effectively primes, or prepares, people to engage in social interaction.

A final line of evidence suggestive of a fundamental social orientation is research on brain activity associated with social pain. Social pain refers to painful feelings experienced related to social loss, rejection or exclusion (Eisenberger, 2012). While people often think of physical and social pain as distinct, neuroscientific research suggests that there is considerable overlap in brain activity associated with these two types of pain, such that both forms of pain appear to draw on the same underlying neurobiological mechanisms (Eisenberger, 2012). This appears to be the case to such an extent that acetaminophen (i.e. Tylenol), a widely available over-the-counter medication for physical pain, has a demonstrable effect on people's neural and behavioral responses to social pain (DeWall et al., 2010). That the brain responds to threats to social "health" in a similar manner to threats to physical health suggests that social connection is deeply important. Collectively, these lines of research provide compelling evidence that social engagement is an important and basic activity in humans.

Evolutionary Basis

Taking an evolutionary perspective, there is good reason to believe this fundamental social orientation is a product of natural selection. Humans' fundamental social orientation has clear connections to cooperation, an important hallmark of our species (West et al., 2011), as well as navigating the challenges of group living. From an evolutionary perspective, cooperative and collaborative behavior offer clear advantages for survival (e.g. Brewer & Caporael, 2006). First, compared to being alone, people working together are physically safer, as individuals can take turns acting as a "sentry", watching for threats, while others engage in daily activities. Closely related, a given individual has a lower probability of being selected as a prey or victim by being one of several in a group (and a group may be less appealing for a predator or rival to attack than a lone individual).

Second, people working together in groups can often accomplish more than one individual alone. Several people together can divide tasks in a way that takes advantage of each individual's expertise, skills, and abilities. Focusing on a single task may also allow people to be more productive, as they minimize the time and cognitive effort involved in switching between different activities (Goldsby et al., 2012).

Finally, people living and working in groups provide a safety net of resources for each other. If one survival-related activity (e.g. hunting) is unsuccessful, people in groups can fall back on the products of other activities undertaken by others (e.g. gathering or growing food). Similarly, if one individual does not know something important (e.g. where to find water; whether a plant is safe to eat; which route is safe), he or she can often turn to others in a group who may know the answer. Individuals living and working alone do not have these additional resources to fall back on in difficult times. Given these considerations, it seems likely that there has been selection for qualities that support cooperative behavior, such as being interested in other people, and motivated to engage with them (Seyfarth & Cheney, 2013)—in other words, having a social orientation.

Working with other people and living in groups also come with challenges that a social orientation can help navigate. First, when working and living in groups, people must pay attention to, and keep track of others. It is also beneficial for them to monitor the relationships that other people have with each other. Knowing who has power or influence over whom, and who likes and dislikes each other—that is, coalition tracking (Barkow et al., 1992)—helps people navigate social situations and minimize conflict. This sort of knowledge can also help people determine whom to align themselves with to maximize resources or benefits.

Second, with cooperation and group living also comes the temptation, and corresponding risk, of people trying to free-ride or cheat—that is, to benefit from others' work without contributing (comparable) work themselves (Barkow et al., 1992; Smith, 2010). Thus, with cooperation and group living comes an increasing need to be able to determine who to trust, to detect deception, and to keep track of peoples' own and others' relationships (with an eye to the intentions and goals of people in those relationships). Thus, evolutionarily, it is in people's interest to notice what others are doing, and to critically evaluate what intentions underlie those actions. Fiske et al. (2007) argued that people have two basic concerns to address when meeting another person: determining that person's intentions (which translate to judgments of warmth) and determining that person's capacity to fulfill those intentions (which translate to judgments of competence). Thinking about others' behavior in this way, and making corresponding judgments, is greatly facilitated by having a mind that endeavors to answer questions about others' intentions and goals—that is, a social orientation.

In short, cooperating with others offers survival advantages, but also additional challenges. As such, it makes sense that individuals who had inclinations, skills, or abilities that facilitated cooperation and the successful navigation of complex social environments would be more likely to survive and reproduce than those who did not. Over time, this would result in selection for traits (cognitive and biological) that support and favor social engagement and interaction, as well as attention to other people's motives and thoughts. We contend that humans' fundamental social orientation as proposed here—which includes social interest, motivation, and skills (e.g. theory of mind, mentalizing)—is a product of these selection processes.

Premise 2: Efficiency

Our second observation is that—all other things being equal—humans have a general predisposition toward *efficiency*. We define efficiency as optimizing energy use, or avoiding unnecessary energy expenditure: that is, minimizing the input that entities provide to attain a given output, or alternatively, maximizing the desired output entities attain for a given input. Here, we wish to emphasize that we make this observation with the caveat of "all other things being equal," recognizing that very frequently, all else is not equal. In a wide range of situations, people may have goals that lead them to engage in cognition or behavior that is highly effortful and/or appears to be quite inefficient. As we underscored in Chapter 1, social interaction is a goal-driven activity, and this is important to keep in mind when analyzing associated behavior. People may do or think things that appear to be quite inefficient; however, they often do so because those actions accomplish a goal they have deemed a high priority. (We address the topic of communicator goals in greater detail in Chapter 6). In the absence of goals or other considerations that direct energy use otherwise, we believe it is reasonable to claim that humans are predisposed to be efficient.

Evidence

A propensity for efficiency in human behavior, and biological systems more generally, has been observed and documented in a variety of sources. For example, researchers have argued that energy efficiency and optimization are guiding principles for the brain's structures and functional operations (Koban et al., 2019; Laughlin & Sejnowski, 2003), and that human brain structure and activity can be viewed in terms of the trade-off between their costs and adaptive benefits (Bullmore & Sporns, 2012). In the domain of sensory systems, scholars have argued that evolution consistently strikes a balance between the information processing gains of sensory systems in animals relative to the energy costs of those systems (Niven & Laughlin, 2008). Similarly, in the domain of motor behavior, researchers have suggested that observations of human and animal motor behavior show coordination of learning and control of movement in ways that optimize energy expenditure for the tasks being performed (Sparrow & Newell, 1998).

In the context of human behavior, a focus on efficiency can translate to people seeking to minimize the amount of energy they use to accomplish their goals—in other words, avoiding wasted effort. In many situations, efficiency is not something people pursue consciously or deliberately, although people certainly can reflect on the energy and resources required for different ways to accomplish goals, and make decisions based on these considerations. In what follows, we offer a few examples of how a predisposition toward efficiency is visible in people's cognition and behavior.

First, we see evidence for a predisposition toward efficiency in the manner in which human thought and action can (and do) shift from explicit to implicit processing over time. Researchers in a range of disciplines have observed that there are two broad "types" or "systems" of processing in human cognition. One processes and responds to input rapidly, outside of conscious awareness (implicit processing; sometimes also referred to as "Type 1" or "System 1"). Another processes and responds to input more slowly, consciously, and reflectively (explicit processing; sometimes also referred to as "Type 2" or "System 2") (e.g. Evans & Stanovich, 2013; Frith & Frith, 2012). Nobel laureate Daniel Kahneman popularized reference to these two systems as "thinking fast and slow," respectively (e.g. Kahneman, 2011). Implicit processing ("thinking fast") is autonomous, unconscious, and relatively effortless; typically, it is not disrupted by increasing people's cognitive load (for example, by asking them to engage in other tasks simultaneously). In contrast, explicit processing ("thinking slow") is controlled, conscious, and relatively effortful; it is disrupted by increases in cognitive load (Evans & Stanovich, 2013).

Some cognitions and behaviors are innately governed by implicit processing (e.g. implicit learning processes; Evans & Stanovich, 2013, p. 236). However, others are governed by implicit processing as a result of well-learned associations. In other words, behaviors or cognitions that are initially controlled and effortful (explicit processing) can become more autonomous and effortless (implicit processing) over time, as a function of practice and experience (e.g. LaRose, 2010). We view this as consistent with a predisposition toward efficiency: when people engage in a thought process or behavior frequently, it is beneficial to expend as little (conscious) energy as possible doing so. This is what we see in human cognition: over time, processing shifts from explicit processing (which requires conscious attention and control, taking attention and, presumably, energy that could be used for other tasks) to implicit processing (which is undertaken automatically, and requires less attention and energy). To the extent that people can engage in implicit, rather than explicit, processing to accomplish their goals, their processing becomes more efficient.

Another domain in which we see a human tendency toward efficiency is in language use and structure (e.g. Regier et al., 2016). One form this takes is the abbreviation of stimuli (e.g. words) people select. This is most famously discussed in Zipf's (1949) law of abbreviation in language, which observes that frequently used words tend to be shorter. Zipf proposed that this was a function of competing demands for efficiency and accuracy in communication; recent research using an artificial (i.e. simulated) language learning paradigm has confirmed that this phenomenon occurs only when both of these demands are present (Kanwal et al., 2017). Piantadosi et al. (2011) demonstrated that the information content of a word (in an information theoretic sense) is an even better predictor of word length than frequency, with more informative words being longer (see also Mahowald et al., 2013). Piantadosi and colleagues argue that this reflects optimization of word length for efficient communication. Studies have also demonstrated that in some cases, both within and across conversations, initial references for objects or ideas (e.g. "the blue rectangular Lego") can become more abbreviated (e.g. "the blue Lego", "the blue one", "blue") over time (e.g. Clark & Krych, 2004). We suggest that this is also consistent with a tendency toward efficiency: once interactants are confident that they can accomplish their goal of communicating effectively with less stimuli (e.g. a shorter phrase or label), they do so, because less stimuli require less energy to produce and process.

A final example of the effects of a predisposition for efficiency on communicative behavior is people's reliance on implicature and inference-making in conversation. Grice (1989) argued convincingly that people's utterances typically imply more meaning than a surface analysis of their text would suggest. Likewise, the audience typically infers more from utterances than is available in a literal analysis of their text. Grice invoked a *cooperative principle* to explain how this occurs. In short, Grice claims that cooperative speakers say only what is necessary to convey the intended meaning to their communicative partners; these communicative partners, in turn, are expected to infer what is not immediately evident in the utterance. In this manner, both communicators are minimizing the energy expended in their communicative behavior, while maximizing its effectiveness (in terms of creating understanding). Similarly, a central tenet of Sperber and Wilson's (1995) *relevance theory*, which addresses how communicators make sense of utterances, is that, "Human cognitive processes ... are geared to achieving the greatest possible cognitive effect for the smallest possible processing effort" (p. vi).

Evolutionary Basis

A predisposition toward efficiency makes evolutionary sense. It is in the interest of living beings to minimize the energy expended for a given outcome: minimizing energy expenditures ensures that people do not waste resources they might need later, or for other endeavors. It seems reasonable to suggest that, in general, people who did not care about wasting energy or resources would be less likely to survive than those who did, as they would have less energy or fewer resources at their disposal to deal with unexpected challenges or hazards. In line with this, Yun et al. (2006) have argued that *return on energy*—the ratio of energy gained to energy expended for that gain—"represents the ultimate basis of competition during evolution" (p. 664). They have proposed that the improvement of return on energy is central to the evolutionary process, potentially even more so than reproductive success.

Premise 3: Predictive Inference-Making

Finally, our third observation is that *predictive inference-making* is a fundamental feature of human mental activity. Predicting the future—that is, what will happen next—is a process that shapes and defines human cognition (e.g. Bar, 2007; Clark, 2013; Friston, 2010; Frith & Frith, 2006; Hutchinson & Barrett, 2019; Rommers et al., 2013; Schacter et al., 2007; Tamir & Thornton, 2018). Generally, people make such predictions via inferences, using available evidence to generate an informed hypothesis or draw a tentative conclusion. Predictive inference-making plays a critical role in reduction and management of uncertainty, which are key activities in human social life (e.g. Afifi & Afifi, 2009; Bach & Dolan, 2012; Brashers, 2001; FeldmanHall & Shenhav, 2019; Gottlieb et al., 2013). In both people's subjective mental experiences and the neural substrates of these experiences, there is compelling evidence for the presence and importance of predictive inference-making.

Evidence

Being able to predict what will happen next plays an important role in people's successful navigation of both social and non-social situations (Clark, 2013). Effective prediction typically draws on learned associations, regularities, and/or patterns. Once people have learned that two things are associated with each other, the presence or actions of one allows them to predict the presence or actions of the other. Infants are capable of associative learning (e.g. Reeb-Sutherland et al., 2012), suggesting that the abilities that underlie prediction are innate in humans.

Learned associations or patterns can become more fully developed as mental models (e.g. Leshinskaya et al., 2020). Here, we use "mental models" as an umbrella term covering a range of systematic, multipart mental representations, including schemas, stereotypes, and "lay" theories; we also note that mental models can include representations of other people's mental processes (which is facilitated by people's social orientation; Premise 1). To the extent that people recognize a given stimulus in context as an exemplar of something for which they have a mental model (i.e. for which they have some kind of a generalized "template"), they can use that model to infer additional properties or characteristics about that stimulus, including how it is likely to change in the future. In this way, mental models provide a platform for predictive inference-making about both traits and states (Frith & Frith, 2006). Thus, prediction renders mental models powerful tools for making sense of the world, and interacting with it.

Focusing specifically on social cognition, there are several ways in which people predict what other people are generally like (traits) or how other people are going to behave in the moment (states), often drawing on mental models (Frith & Frith, 2006; Tamir & Thornton, 2018). Identifying people as members of social groups allows people to use group-based stereotypes to make inferences about both characteristics and behaviors (Frith & Frith, 2006; Giles, 2012; Hogg, 2000; Turner et al., 1987). At the individual level, knowledge of other people's personality traits (e.g. being introverted or extraverted) or idiosyncratic characteristics can be used to predict people's behavior and preferences (Frith & Frith, 2006; Tamir & Thornton, 2018). It is important to emphasize that people's predictions based on stereotypes, personality traits, or individuated knowledge may be incorrect. The critical point is that people can and do make these predictions. As discussed below, making predictions that are sometimes erroneous is likely to still be more adaptive than making no predictions at all.

There is also a growing body of theoretical and empirical research suggesting that prediction is a fundamental feature of how the human brain functions (e.g. Barrett & Simmons, 2015; Friston 2009, 2010). Recently, it has been proposed that much of human brain function can be explained by conceptualizing the brain as a system that generates predictions about its experiences, and seeks to minimize prediction error (quantified, following some simplifying assumptions, as *free energy*[2] in theoretical neuroscience) based on the feedback it gets (FeldmanHall & Shenhav, 2019; Friston 2009, 2010). Much of this work is grounded in the *Bayesian brain hypothesis* and/or a predictive coding framework (e.g. Shamay-Tsoory et al., 2019).

According to the Bayesian brain hypothesis, the brain has an internal, generative model of the world that describes the causes of sensory input probabilistically. Perception can be described as a process in which the brain makes predictions about sensory experiences based on this generative model, then checks these predictions against input from the senses. Errors in prediction (i.e. differences found between the brain's prediction and sensory input) provide data that is used to update the generative model. Through this process of comparing predictions and sensory input, and updating the model to address discrepancies, the brain's generative model of the world is optimized for accuracy over time. As described by Friston (2010), this hypothesis views the brain as "an inference machine that actively predicts and explains its sensations" (p. 129). In this, predictive inference-making is an essential and fundamental mechanism in the brain function and activity.[3]

Predictive inference-making is also visible in a range of different communicative behaviors. For instance, people anticipate what their partners will say in conversation, to such an extent that they can often complete their partners' sentences before those sentences are verbalized (e.g. Pickering & Garrod, 2013). Similarly, people often draw relatively accurate conclusions about what someone is arguing or talking about before they finish speaking. People anticipate each other's physical movements in ways that allow them to interact and move together. People also predict, with reasonable accuracy, when someone will finish speaking, which allows rapid exchanges and turn-taking with minimal gaps in live conversation (Levinson, 2006).

Evolutionary Basis

From an evolutionary perspective, being able to generate internal models of one's environment and to predict what will happen next based on those models should be advantageous. Specifically, this ability helps people to reduce and/or manage uncertainty in their environment (FeldmanHall & Shenhav, 2019). Accurately predicting what will happen next allows people to optimize their own actions in that environment, so they can enact what would best help them survive (Bruineberg et al., 2018).

Being able to predict impending changes in their environment also reduces people's uncertainty about the future, and the corresponding energy people spend considering multiple, possible events or outcomes they may have to face (Clark, 2013; Friston & Frith, 2015; Frith & Frith, 2006). Thus, accurate prediction also helps people optimize the energy they use to determine what is happening in a situation and select an appropriate response (rather than spending energy guessing at what will happen, and preparing multiple responses that will not all be used). As discussed above (Premise 2), optimizing the energy used to accomplish one's goals—that is, being efficient—should offer a survival advantage. Consequently, we argue that a basic tendency toward efficiency also underlies or supports the human propensity for prediction and inference-making based on mental models.

Summary

In this chapter, we have shown that human beings can be characterized as fundamentally social in orientation, that human mental processes are governed by a predisposition for efficiency, and that predictive inference-making is a core feature of human mental activity. We believe that these are general observations about human behavior; that is, they are not specific to activities or processes related to communication or creating understanding. However, they are sufficiently fundamental to human nature that they underlie the process of creating understanding. As such, we treat them as a foundation (i.e. premises) that helps support, and by extension explain, the more specific endeavors involved in creating understanding. We now turn our attention to these specifics.

Notes

1. We show this film in our undergraduate course on understanding, and ask our students to engage in a similar task. Without fail, we replicate these results each semester.
2. It should be noted that in Friston's theorizing, the term "free energy" refers to an information theoretic quantity, roughly analogous to uncertainty. Our usage of the term "energy" in all other parts of this chapter refers to metabolic energy.
3. It should be noted that there is also a formal, computational component to the Bayesian brain hypothesis, as well as related constructs such as the *free energy principle,* that describes these phenomena mathematically. Such content is outside the scope of this book, but we encourage interested readers to see Friston (2009, 2010) for an introduction to the computational components, as well as additional resources on this topic.

References

Afifi, T. D., & Afifi, W. A. (Eds.) (2009). *Uncertainty, information management, and disclosure decisions: Theories and applications.* Routledge. https://doi.org/10.4324/9780203933046

Apperly, I. (2018). Mindreading and psycholinguistic approaches to perspective taking: Establishing common ground. *Topics in Cognitive Science, 10*(1), 133–139. https://doi.org/10.1111/tops.12308

Bach, D. R., & Dolan, R. J. (2012). Knowing how much you don't know: A neural organization of uncertainty estimates. *Nature Reviews Neuroscience, 13*(8), 572–586. https://doi.org/10.1038/nrn3289

Bar, M. (2007). The proactive brain: Using analogies and associations to generate predictions. *Trends in Cognitive Sciences, 11*(7), 280–289. https://doi.org/10.1016/j.tics.2007.05.005

Barkow, J. H., Cosmides, L., & Tooby, J. (Eds.). (1992). *The adapted mind: Evolutionary psychology and the generation of culture*. Oxford University Press.

Baron-Cohen, S. (1997). *Mindblindness: An essay on autism and theory of mind*. MIT Press.

Barrett, L. F., & Simmons, W. K. (2015). Interoceptive predictions in the brain. *Nature Reviews Neuroscience, 16*(7), 419–429. https://doi.org/10.1038/nrn3950

Binder, J., Frost, J., Hammeke, T., Bellgowan, P., Rao, S., & Cox, R. (1999). Conceptual processing during the conscious resting state. A functional MRI study. *Journal of Cognitive Neuroscience, 11*, 80–95. https://doi.org/10.1162/089892999563265

Brashers, D. E. (2001). Communication and uncertainty management. *Journal of Communication, 51*(3), 477–497. https://doi.org/10.1111/j.1460-2466.2001.tb02892.x

Brewer, M. B., & Caporael, L. R. (2006). An evolutionary perspective on social identity: Revisiting groups. In M. Schaller, J. A. Simpson, & D.T. Kenrick (Eds.), *Evolution and social psychology* (pp. 143–161). Psychology Press.

Bruineberg, J., Kiverstein, J., & Rietveld, E. (2018). The anticipating brain is not a scientist: the free-energy principle from an ecological-enactive perspective. *Synthese, 195*(6), 2417–2444. https://doi.org/10.1007/s11229-016-1239-1

Bullmore, E., & Sporns, O. (2012). The economy of brain network organization. *Nature Reviews Neuroscience, 13*(5), 336–349. https://doi.org/10.1038/nrn3214

Cacioppo, J. T., & Cacioppo, S. (2014). Social relationships and health: The toxic effects of perceived social isolation. *Social and Personality Psychology Compass, 8*(2), 58–72. https://doi.org/10.1111/spc3.12087

Chevallier, C., Kohls, G., Troiani, V., Brodkin, E. S., & Schultz, R. T. (2012). The social motivation theory of autism. *Trends in Cognitive Sciences, 16*(4), 231–239. https://doi.org/10.1016/j.tics.2012.02.007

Clark, A. (2013). Whatever next? Predictive brains, situated agents, and the future of cognitive science. *Behavioral and Brain Sciences, 36*(3), 181–204. https://doi.org/10.1017/S0140525X12000477

Clark, H. H., & Krych, M. A. (2004). Speaking while monitoring addressees for understanding. *Journal of Memory and Language, 50*(1), 62–81. https://doi.org/10.1016/j.jml.2003.08.004

Cohen, A. S., & German, T. C. (2010). A reaction time advantage for calculating beliefs over public representations signals domain specificity for 'theory of mind'. *Cognition, 115*(3), 417–425. https://doi.org/10.1016/j.cognition.2010.03.001

Cohen, A. S., Sasaki, J. Y., & German, T. C. (2015). Specialized mechanisms for theory of mind: Are mental representations special because they are mental or because they are representations?. *Cognition, 136*, 49–63. https://doi.org/10.1016/j.cognition.2014.11.016

Cohen, S. (2004). Social relationships and health. *American Psychologist, 59*(8), 676–684. https://doi.org/10.1037/0003-066X.59.8.676

Dennett, D. C. (1987). *The intentional stance*. MIT Press.

Dennett, D. C. (2017). *From bacteria to Bach and back: The evolution of minds*. W. W. Norton & Company.

DeWall, C. N., MacDonald, G., Webster, G. D., Masten, C. L., Baumeister, R. F., Powell, C., Combs, D., Schurtz, D. R., Stillman, T. F., Tice, D. M., & Eisenberger, N. I. (2010). Acetaminophen reduces social pain: Behavioral and neural evidence. *Psychological Science, 21*(7), 931–937. https://doi.org/10.1177/0956797610374741

Dunbar, R. I. (2004). Gossip in evolutionary perspective. *Review of General Psychology, 8*(2), 100–110. https://doi.org/10.1037/1089-2680.8.2.100

Eisenberger, N. I. (2012). The pain of social disconnection: examining the shared neural underpinnings of physical and social pain. *Nature Reviews Neuroscience, 13*(6), 421–434. https://doi.org/10.1038/nrn3231

Evans, J. S. B., & Stanovich, K. E. (2013). Dual-process theories of higher cognition: Advancing the debate. *Perspectives on Psychological Science, 8(3),* 223–241. https://doi.org/10.1177/1745691612460685

FeldmanHall, O., & Shenhav, A. (2019). Resolving uncertainty in a social world. *Nature Human Behaviour, 3*(5), 426–435. https://doi.org/10.1038/s41562-019-0590-x

Fiske, S. T., Cuddy, A. J., & Glick, P. (2007). Universal dimensions of social cognition: Warmth and competence. *Trends in Cognitive Sciences, 11*(2), 77–83. https://doi.org/10.1016/j.tics.2006.11.005

Friston, K. (2009). The free-energy principle: a rough guide to the brain?. *Trends in Cognitive Sciences, 13*(7), 293–301. https://doi.org/10.1016/j.tics.2009.04.005

Friston, K. (2010). The free-energy principle: a unified brain theory?. *Nature Reviews Neuroscience, 11*(2), 127–138. https://doi.org/10.1038/nrn2787

Friston, K. J., & Frith, C. D. (2015). Active inference, communication and hermeneutics. *Cortex, 68,* 129–143. https://doi.org/10.1016/j.cortex.2015.03.025

Frith, C. D., & Frith, U. (2005). Theory of mind. *Current Biology, 15*(17), R644-R645. https://doi.org/10.1016/j.cub.2005.08.041

Frith, C. D., & Frith, U. (2006). How we predict what other people are going to do. *Brain Research, 1079*(1), 36–46. https://doi.org/10.1016/j.brainres.2005.12.126

Frith, C. D., & Frith, U. (2012). Mechanisms of social cognition. *Annual Review of Psychology, 63*(1), 287–313. https://doi.org/10.1146/annurev-psych-120710-100449

Giles, H. (Ed.). (2012). *The handbook of intergroup communication.* Routledge. https://doi.org/10.4324/9780203148624

Goldsby, H. J., Dornhaus, A., Kerr, B., & Ofria, C. (2012). Task-switching costs promote the evolution of division of labor and shifts in individuality. *Proceedings of the National Academy of Sciences, 109*(34), 13686–13691. https://doi.org/10.1073/pnas.1202233109

Gottlieb, J., Oudeyer, P. Y., Lopes, M., & Baranes, A. (2013). Information-seeking, curiosity, and attention: computational and neural mechanisms. *Trends in Cognitive Sciences, 17*(11), 585–593. https://doi.org/10.1016/j.tics.2013.09.001

Greicius, M. D., Krasnow, B., Reiss, A. L., & Menon, V. (2003). Functional connectivity in the resting brain: a network analysis of the default mode hypothesis. *Proceedings of the National Academy of Sciences, 100*(1), 253–258. https://doi.org/10.1073/pnas.0135058100

Grice, H. P. (1989). *Studies in the way of words.* Harvard University Press.

Heider, F., & Simmel, M. (1944). An experimental study of apparent behavior. *The American Journal of Psychology, 57*(2), 243–259. https://doi.org/10.2307/1416950

Heyes, C. (2014). Submentalizing: I am not really reading your mind. *Perspectives on Psychological Science, 9*(2), 131–143. https://doi.org/10.1177/1745691613518076

Hogg, M. A. (2000). Subjective uncertainty reduction through self-categorization: A motivational theory of social identity processes. *European Review of Social Psychology, 11*(1), 223–255. https://doi.org/10.1080/14792772043000040

Holt-Lunstad, J., Smith, T. B., & Layton, J. B. (2010). Social relationships and mortality risk: A meta-analytic review. *PLOS Medicine, 7*(7), Article e1000316. https://doi.org/10.1371/journal.pmed.1000316

Hutchinson, J. B., & Barrett, L. F. (2019). The power of predictions: An emerging paradigm for psychological research. *Current Directions in Psychological Science, 28*(3), 280–291. https://doi.org/10.1177%2F0963721419831992

Kahneman, D. (2011). *Thinking, fast and slow*. Farrar, Straus and Giroux.

Kanwal, J., Smith, K., Culbertson, J., & Kirby, S. (2017). Zipf's law of abbreviation and the principle of least effort: Language users optimise a miniature lexicon for efficient communication. *Cognition, 165*, 45–52. https://doi.org/10.1016/j.cognition.2017.05.001

Kato, M., & Mugitani, R. (2015). Pareidolia in infants. *PLOS ONE 10*(2), Article e0118539. https://doi.org/10.1371/journal.pone.0118539

Koban, L., Ramamoorthy, A., & Konvalinka, I. (2019). Why do we fall into sync with others? Interpersonal synchronization and the brain's optimization principle. *Social Neuroscience, 14*(1), 1–9. https://doi.org/10.1080/17470919.2017.1400463

LaRose, R. (2010). The problem of media habits, *Communication Theory*, 20(2), 194–222. https://doi.org/10.1111/j.1468-2885.2010.01360.x

Laughlin, S. B., & Sejnowski, T. J. (2003). Communication in neuronal networks. *Science, 301*(5641), 1870–1874. https://doi.org/10.1126/science.1089662

Leshinskaya, A., Bajaj, M., & Thompson-Schill, S. L. (2020). Incidental binding between predictive relations. *Cognition, 199*, Article 104238. https://doi.org/10.1016/j.cognition.2020.104238

Levinson, S. C. (2006). On the human "interaction engine". In N. J. Enfield & S. C. Levinson, *Roots of human sociality: Culture, cognition, and interaction* (pp. 39–69). Berg.

Lieberman, M. D. (2013). *Social: Why our brains are wired to connect*. Broadway Books.

Liu, J., Li, J., Feng, L., Li, L., Tian, J., & Lee, K. (2014). Seeing Jesus in toast: Neural and behavioral correlates of face pareidolia. *Cortex, 53*, 60–77. https://doi.org/10.1016/j.cortex.2014.01.013

Mahowald, K., Fedorenko, E., Piantadosi, S. T., & Gibson, E. (2013). Info/information theory: Speakers choose shorter words in predictive contexts. *Cognition, 126*(2), 313–318. https://doi.org/10.1016/j.cognition.2012.09.010

Niven, J. E., & Laughlin, S. B. (2008). Energy limitation as a selective pressure on the evolution of sensory systems. *The Journal of Experimental Biology, 211*, 1792–1804. https://doi.org/10.1242/jeb.017574

Piantadosi, S. T., Tily, H., & Gibson, E. (2011). Word lengths are optimized for efficient communication. *Proceedings of the National Academy of Sciences, 108*(9), 3526–3529. https://doi.org/10.1073/pnas.1012551108

Pickering, M. J., & Garrod, S. (2013). An integrated theory of language production and comprehension. *Behavioral and Brain Sciences, 36*(4), 329–347. https://doi.org/10.1017/S0140525X12001495

Reeb-Sutherland, B. C., Levitt, P., & Fox, N. A. (2012). The predictive nature of individual differences in early associative learning and emerging social behavior. *PLOS ONE, 7*(1), Article e30511. https://doi.org/10.1371/journal.pone.0030511

Regier, T., Carstensen, A., & Kemp, C. (2016). Languages support efficient communication about the environment: Words for snow revisited. *PLOS ONE, 11*(4), Article e0151138. https://doi.org/10.1371/journal.pone.0151138

Rommers, J., Meyer, A. S., Praamstra, P., & Huettig, F. (2013). The contents of predictions in sentence comprehension: Activation of the shape of objects before they are referred to. *Neuropsychologia, 51*(3), 437–447. https://doi.org/10.1016/j.neuropsychologia.2012.12.002

Rosset, E. (2008). It's no accident: Our bias for intentional explanations. *Cognition, 108*(3), 771–780. https://doi.org/10.1016/j.cognition.2008.07.001

Schacter, D. L., Addis, D. R., & Buckner, R. L. (2007). Remembering the past to imagine the future: the prospective brain. *Nature Reviews Neuroscience, 8*(9), 657–661. https://doi.org/10.1038/nrn2213

Scott-Phillips, T. C. (2015). *Speaking our minds: Why human communication is different, and how language evolved to make it special.* Palgrave Macmillan.

Seyfarth, R. M., & Cheney, D. L. (2013). Affiliation, empathy, and the origins of theory of mind. *Proceedings of the National Academy of Sciences, 110*(Supplement 2), 10349–10356. https://doi.org/10.1073/pnas.1301223110

Shamay-Tsoory, S. G., Saporta, N., Marton-Alper, I. Z., & Gvirts, H. Z. (2019). Herding brains: A core neural mechanism for social alignment. *Trends in Cognitive Sciences, 23*(3), 174–186. https://doi.org/10.1016/j.tics.2019.01.002

Smith, E. A. (2010). Communication and collective action: Language and the evolution of human cooperation. *Evolution and Human Behavior, 31*(4), 231–245. https://doi.org/10.1016/j.evolhumbehav.2010.03.001

Sparrow, W. A., & Newall, K. M. (1998). Metabolic energy expenditure and the regulation of movement economy. *Psychonomic Bulletin and Review, 5*(2), 173–196. https://doi.org/10.3758/BF03212943

Sperber, D., & Wilson, D. (1995). *Relevance: Communication and cognition (2nd Ed.).* Blackwell.

Spunt, R. P., Meyer, M. L., & Lieberman, M. D. (2015). The default mode of human brain function primes the intentional stance. *Journal of Cognitive Neuroscience, 27*(6), 1116–1124. http://doi.org/10.1162/jocn_a_00785

Tamir, D. I., & Thornton, M. A. (2018). Modeling the predictive social mind. *Trends in Cognitive Sciences, 22*(3), 201–212. https://doi.org/10.1016/j.tics.2017.12.005

Turner, J. C., Hogg, M. A., Oakes, P. J., Reicher, S. D., & Wetherell, M. S. (1987). A self-categorization theory. *Rediscovering the social group: A self-categorization theory* (pp. 42–66). Basil Blackwell.

Umberson, D., Crosnoe, R., & Reczek, C. (2010). Social relationships and health behavior across the life course. *Annual Review of Sociology, 36*, 139–157. https://doi.org/10.1146/annurev-soc-070308-120011

West, S. A., El Mouden, C., & Gardner, A. (2011). Sixteen common misconceptions about the evolution of cooperation in humans. *Evolution and Human Behavior, 32*, 231–262. http://doi.org/10.1016/j.evolhumbehav.2010.08.001

Yang, Y. C., Boen, C., Gerken, K., Li, T., Schorpp, K., & Harris, K. M. (2015). Social relationships and physiological determinants of longevity across the human life span. *Proceedings of the National Academy of Sciences, 113*(3), 578–583. http://doi.org/10.1073/pnas.1511085112

Yun, A. J., Lee, P. Y., Doux, J. D., & Conley, B. R. (2006). A general theory of evolution based on energy efficiency: Its implications for diseases. *Medical Hypotheses, 66*(3), 664–670. https://doi.org/10.1016/j.mehy.2005.07.002

Zipf, G. K. (1949). *Human behavior and the principle of least effort: An introduction to human ecology*. Addison-Wesley Press.

CHAPTER FOUR

Components of Communicating

This chapter outlines key components of human communication. We first describe how people initiate ostensive communicative interactions. Next, we argue that once an interaction is initiated, people implicitly treat the process of communicating as a cooperative endeavor. We then articulate the interactional consequences of communicative cooperation. Finally, we address how the stimuli that people present in interaction activate specific meme states in their interlocutors' minds, proposing a process in which communicators generate and test predictions about what will occur next in interaction. These components of communicating—initiating interaction, cooperating communicatively, and activating meme states— will serve as building blocks for our model of creating understanding, which we present in the next chapter.

In the previous two chapters, we laid a foundation for theorizing about how people create understanding. First, we conceptualized understanding as a state in which people experience entrainment of their mental states as a result of (ostensive) use of social stimuli—that is, of communicating. We then presented a set of observations about the fundamental nature of humans' brains and behavior that we contend underlie and guide social interaction. With this foundation laid, we now turn our attention to the process of communicating itself. In this chapter, we build on the premises we have established, in conjunction with extant models of ostensive-inferential communication (e.g. Sperber & Wilson, 1995) to describe key components of communicating, with a focus on their mechanics.

Ostensive-inferential models propose that communication consists of communicators making inferences (hence the name) about what the other is thinking or intending based on evidence provided in context. We believe this conceptualization of the process of communication is the best available theoretical alternative to code models. In what follows, this depiction of communication serves as the backbone for our explanation of several components of social interaction; these components will ultimately serve as building blocks for modeling how people create understanding.

Initiating Interactions: Mentalizing and Intentions

To be able to explain how people create understanding in interaction, we first have to address how people come to interact in communicative situations—that is, how people initiate ostensive communication. As a starting point, we look to people's capacity for mentally representing not only their own ideas and thoughts, but also those of others.

As discussed in Chapter 3, people are capable of *mentalizing*, or inferring what others are thinking (e.g. Apperly, 2018; O'Grady et al., 2015). People also have the capacity to represent how others represent thoughts and ideas. Adapting terminology from O'Grady and colleagues (2015), we use the term *recursive mentalizing* to refer to people's capacity to "embed further levels of mental representation inside existing mental representations" (p. 313). For example, people can think things like, "Sally knows the meeting is on Friday" (*mentalizing*), but also "Sally believes that Anne doesn't know the meeting is on Friday" (*recursive mentalizing*). Experimental research by O'Grady et al. (2015) has demonstrated that people can represent and track up to seven levels of embedding of others' thoughts. There is a considerable body of work in developmental psychology, cognitive psychology, and related fields (in addition to our daily lived experiences) that supports the existence of humans' capacities for mentalizing and recursive mentalizing (e.g. Scott-Phillips, 2015).

We consider these social cognitive skills and abilities to be manifestations of humans' fundamental social orientation (Chapter 3: Premise 1). As we discussed in the previous chapter, this social orientation provides a lens through which people experience and interpret human behavior. In particular, people assume that mental states are the basis for what other people do. This tendency to see people's actions in terms of intentions and goals is often discussed as a component of "lay" psychological theory (e.g. Heider, 1958/2013; Heider & Simmel, 1944); others have considered it an aspect of theory of mind (Frith & Frith, 2005). There is experimental evidence demonstrating that people make inferences about intentionality and motives—effectively, others' mental states—rapidly and automatically when they perceive and evaluate behavior (Hassin et al., 2005; Malle & Holbrook, 2012; Smith & Miller, 1983). Indeed, people do this to such an extent that some scholars have argued that people treat and experience such inferences simply as observations about the world, rather than as subjective interpretations (Sillars, 1998).

We propose that the link that people perceive between social stimuli (i.e. behavior) and meme states (i.e. mental states) allows us to explain how people initiate and engage in ostensive communication (Ciaramidaro et al., 2014)—that is, interactions in which people make manifest their intentions to communicate something specific (Sperber & Wilson, 1995). Scholars have argued that ostensive human communication requires the presentation and recognition of two different types of intentions: communicative and informative intentions. *Communicative intentions* address a person's desire to communicate. *Informative intentions* address the content that a person wants to communicate (Scott-Phillips, 2015; Sperber & Wilson, 1995).

Before a person can communicate any kind of content—that is, before that person's informative intentions can be recognized as such—other people must first recognize that this person is intending to communicate at all. People do many things every day that result in presenting many different types of stimuli to the rest of the world. However, a majority of these presentations of stimuli are not intended to have communicative value—they are incidental by-products of living and acting in the world. For example, when people walk down a street, their legs and arms move (as they propel themselves forward) and their gaze moves around (taking in their surroundings). Most of the time, this behavior is not intended to activate any specific meme states in anyone, though it may do so. (For instance, someone might see such a person walking down the street and think, "That woman is enjoying her walk"). However, if someone sees his friend as he walks down the street, locks eyes with her, and starts moving in a visibly purposeful way toward that friend, he could *intend* his behavior to *communicate* to her: "I see you; I am coming over to say hello to you." In the first example, there is no communicative intention associated with body movement and gaze; in the second, there is a communicative intention associated with body movement and gaze. When communicators initiate an interaction, their communicative intention is that their "audience recognize[s] *that* [they] are trying to communicate" (Scott-Phillips, 2015, p. 26). For this to be successful, that audience must recognize, or infer, that someone wants to communicate with them.

It is worth emphasizing that communicators may not always fully "agree" on what stimuli are presented ostensively, and thus what stimuli they should attend to when making inferences about either communicative or informative intentions. Communicators may present stimuli with the intention that it be recognized as ostensive and communicative, and their interlocutors may not recognize those stimuli as such. For example, someone might use a particular tone of voice with the informative intention of conveying sarcasm, but his interlocutor might not recognize this (and therefore ignore tone as pertinent social stimuli). Similarly, communicators may interpret and treat some stimuli as ostensive and communicative that were not intended as such. For example, someone might see an interlocutor's lack of eye contact as an intentional indication of disinterest, when that interlocutor is simply shy (and thus avoids eye contact by default, with no informative intention behind it). As long as the process of interaction is not seriously disrupted by these mismatches, communicators are unlikely to realize they occurred, and the overall process of creating understanding should be relatively unaffected. If and when such a mismatch in classifying stimuli is detected, however, communicators will likely need to engage in disambiguation and/or error correction processes (which we discuss in greater detail below, and in Chapter 6).

In sum, we propose that people's capacity for mentalizing and their assumption that mental states are the basis for social behavior are what allow them to recognize stimuli as evidence of communicative and informative intentions (e.g. Ciaramidaro et al., 2014). Because of their capacity for recursive mentalizing, communicators are also implicitly aware that other people process social stimuli as evidence of mental states. This awareness enables people to intentionally present stimuli as evidence of their communicative and informative intentions, and to recognize other's behavior accordingly (Scott-Phillips, 2015). Together, these abilities allow people to initiate ostensive interactions by enacting behaviors like eye contact, uptake of breath, or hand gestures as indications that they would like to communicate, and for other people to recognize these behaviors as means to that end.

Communicative Cooperation and Interaction

Once a communicative intention is recognized and people initiate an ostensive, communicative interaction, we contend that people implicitly approach the process of communicating as a *cooperative* endeavor (Clark, 1996; Grice, 1989; Levinson, 2006; Sperber & Wilson, 1995). In both lay and scholarly usage, the term "cooperation" can refer to several different phenomena. Scott-Phillips (2015) identifies three different types of cooperation involved in human interaction: *communicative cooperation, informative cooperation,* and *material cooperation*. Before proceeding, we think it is helpful to briefly distinguish these different types, and clarify which we intend to focus on.

The first type of cooperation that Scott-Phillips (2015) identifies, *communicative cooperation*, consists of using stimuli in a way that enables or facilitates communication. This includes (but is not limited to) exhibiting and observing stimuli in interpretable or conventional ways, and using established communication systems (i.e. "codes"). For example, speaking at a sufficiently audible volume or using words that fellow communicators know in a conventional way are instances of communicative cooperation. Conversely, speaking so quietly that one cannot be heard, using words others do not know, or using words in unconventional ways (e.g. saying "dog" to index a plant) are all acts that could be seen as communicatively uncooperative. In both everyday interaction and theorizing about communication, people often take communicative cooperation for granted—that is, they presume that others are using stimuli in a conventional manner, and that others are acting in ways that facilitate the creation of understanding (e.g. that they are not saying "dog" to mean "plant"). However, when miscommunication or communicative "failures" occur, such outcomes can often be traced to problems with communicative cooperation, which can be intentional or unintentional.

The second type of cooperation, *informative cooperation*, consists of providing evidence for inferences (i.e. stimuli to activate meme states) in an honest and truthful manner (as in Grice's conversational maxim of *quality*). Essentially, this is acting in good faith as a communicator: offering stimuli that accurately reflect the meme states one has in mind, and that do not deliberately mislead other communicators. This type of cooperation focuses on the content that is communicated, and its truth value. Saying, "I'm upset" when one is feeling upset is an example of informatively cooperative behavior (i.e. one is making a truthful statement about one's emotional state). Saying "I'm fine" when one is feeling upset in order to hide one's true emotional state is an example of behavior that is not informatively cooperative (i.e. one is making a deceptive or untruthful statement about one's emotional state). Generally, what constitutes "truth" is grounded in a given communicator's perspective: if they are expressing something they believe to be true (even if, objectively, it is incorrect), their behavior is considered informatively cooperative. Thus, if Sally says, "The store opens at 10:00" believing the store does indeed open at 10:00, she is acting in an informatively cooperative manner even if the store actually opens at 11:00. (She is just mistaken about the truth value of her beliefs about the store's hours). Typically, people assume their interlocutors are being informatively cooperative (e.g. Levine, 2014), unless they have evidence suggesting otherwise.

The third type of cooperation, *material cooperation*, consists of acting in ways that pursue or promote prosocial goals. When people practice material cooperation, they are doing things that are considered helpful, positive, or supportive for others. This is the type of cooperation that most closely matches everyday (lay) use of the term "cooperation". Answering a question, complying with a request, offering assistance, or complimenting someone are all materially cooperative behaviors (i.e. they help others, or are actions with prosocial goals and outcomes). Ignoring a question, failing to comply with a request, denying assistance, or insulting someone are all materially uncooperative behaviors (i.e. they do not help others, or are actions with antisocial goals and outcomes).

These three types of cooperation can occur in different combinations. For instance, it is possible to be communicatively cooperative but informatively and materially uncooperative: telling a lie, in a way that someone can clearly understand, in order to hurt that person's feelings, is an example of this combination. Similarly, it is possible to be communicatively and materially cooperative, but informatively uncooperative: telling a lie, in a way someone can clearly understand, to save face or protect that person's feelings is an example of this combination. It is even possible to be informatively and materially cooperative, but communicatively uncooperative: this can happen, for example, when a technician or specialist offers accurate and truthful advice for addressing a problem, but does so using terminology or jargon the people they are talking with do not know (e.g. Shulman et al., 2020).

To successfully create understanding, we contend, the only form of cooperation strictly required is communicative cooperation. Without this, it would be effectively impossible for people to make accurate inferences (or have any chance at being close). Even when communicators disagree about aspects of the content they address (such as holding opposing viewpoints), or differ in their higher order social or relational goals (as occurs in conflict or deception), they still generally seek to create understanding at the level of communicative processes (Levinson, 2006; Scott-Phillips, 2015). With that said, in most circumstances, creating understanding also involves informative cooperation. (We address situations in which communicators are not informatively cooperative, such as engaging in deception, in Chapter 6). In what follows, we focus on the consequences of communicative cooperation for the process of creating understanding.

First, once people consent to communicate—and thus, to communicatively cooperate—they *jointly attend* to the interaction; that is, interactants pay attention to the stimuli each person presents. (We do emphasize, however, that the degree of attention may differ between interactants, as a function of their goals, interest, and abilities). Joint attention to stimuli in interaction is necessary for communicators' perception and processing of those stimuli. If interactants did not attend to each other's stimuli, there would be no shared physical basis for communication.

Second, once people consent to communicate—and thus, to communicatively cooperate—they assume they are collectively pursuing a *shared goal of creating understanding* (Aune et al., 2005). This assumption leads communicators to look to social stimuli that interlocutors present as evidence of the meme states, and by extension, situation models that those interlocutors have in mind (i.e. as evidence of informative intentions). As a result of this shared goal, communicators can also use stimuli in ways that they believe will activate the meme states they desire or intend in their interlocutors' minds (Grice, 1989; Scott-Phillips, 2015; Sperber & Wilson, 1995).

Third, and closely related, communicators treat the stimuli that each person presents as *relevant* to their interaction and their mutual goal of creating understanding, and process these stimuli accordingly. The importance of relevance to communicative processes was famously addressed by Grice (1975), who proposed "be relevant" as a maxim of conversation. Subsequently, Sperber and Wilson (1995) further developed the concept of *relevance* in their *relevance theory*. In the theory, *relevance* is defined as the trade-off between *processing effort* and *positive cognitive effects* related to a stimulus. Processing effort refers to the energy required to process a set of stimuli, leading to the activation of meme states. Positive cognitive effects refers to the change in mental representations—that is, in our terminology, the activation of meme states and/or ultimately, changes in a situation model—that result from processing a given set of stimuli (Sperber & Wilson, 1995). Our use of *relevance* follows this definition (which, we note, is essentially anchored in considerations of efficiency; Chapter 3: Premise 2).

Sperber and Wilson (1995) argue convincingly that considerations of relevance guide both cognition and behavior when people communicate. In their *cognitive principle*—which we paraphrase here using the terminology we have introduced—they propose communicators choose and use the stimuli they believe to be most relevant to their interlocutors, given the meme states that those communicators seek to activate. The stimuli that communicators perceive, in turn, activate the most relevant meme states available to them via inferential processes. (We present our account of the nature of these processes below).

In this, it is important to highlight that inferential processes are not necessarily conscious or deliberate; they may be, and often are, unconscious and unintentional. Sperber and Wilson (1995) emphasize that the maximization of relevance via such inferential processes they describe is not a conscious choice or decision;

it is simply how human cognition operates. Following from this, they propose in their *communicative principle* that the act of communicating implies that communicators (a) believe the stimuli they are providing are relevant; and (b) should assume that the stimuli other communicators are providing are relevant (to the extent possible in the broader circumstances of the interaction). Drawing on this work, we propose that when people are acting in communicatively cooperative ways, their thoughts and actions are generally guided by these principles of relevance.

Finally, we propose that once people consent to communicate—and thus, to communicatively cooperate—they track each other's knowledge and beliefs in interaction. We wish to emphasize that this is not necessarily a conscious or mindful undertaking; rather, it appears to be something people do spontaneously at a basic level, and sometimes do more deliberately at higher levels (e.g. Apperly & Butterfill, 2009). There is empirical evidence that people both implicitly and explicitly track what they believe their interlocutors know (e.g. Apperly, 2018; Apperly & Butterfill, 2009; Schneider et al., 2015). What others know (and are known to know) is both dynamic and enduring. Both person's knowledge and other people's mental representations of that knowledge can be changed, or updated, via the process of communication (Clark, 1996). In this way, they are dynamic. People's representations of others' knowledge or beliefs also persist across time in communicators' memory, within and across interactions. In this way, they are enduring; communicators retain a record of what has been established and communicated in the past with specific interlocutors. This record is then available (i.e. may be activated or recalled) when the communicators interact with those interlocutors at different points in time. As we describe in the following section, this can potentially influence what meme states are activated by the stimuli communicators present and process.

Meme State Activation in Interaction

In Chapter 2, we established that stimuli can activate meme states. We now address how this occurs—that is, how a given stimulus comes to activate a particular meme state. In this, we begin with the foundational assumption that stimuli and memes can be reliably associated in people's minds (see Chapter 2). Drawing on scholarship on learning and memory (e.g. Henke, 2010; Rudmann, 2018), we first discuss how such associations form, and how they can explain meme state activation when stimuli are presented in literal or highly conventional ways. We then address meme state activation in more complex situations, in which communicators must make inferences based on potentially ambiguous stimuli.

Associations Between Stimuli and Memes

Associations between stimuli and memes can be established (i.e. *encoded*, in the terminology of memory research) in different ways. In some cases, people encode associations between stimuli and single (unitized) memes via repeated exposure. This is what occurs in associative learning, such as classical conditioning or semantic memory (Henke, 2010). For instance, when learning a language, people spend a great deal of time learning vocabulary, or the associations between combinations of auditory stimuli (sounds or phonemes for spoken language), or visual stimuli (words and/or characters for written language), and corresponding memes (i.e. conceptual definitions of words). Speakers of different languages associate different auditory and visual stimuli with the same meme (e.g. spoken and written "dog", "perro", and "inu/犬" with the concept of "canine animal" for English, Spanish, and Japanese speakers, respectively). Similarly, through their everyday experiences, people come to associate sensory input like sounds, smells, and tastes with specific concepts like a bird song, sulfur, and chocolate chip cookies (respectively). Often, these associations are learned implicitly as opposed to explicitly (or effortfully), though learning can occur through either route.

People can also encode a set of associations between stimuli and multiple memes from a single experience (as in episodic memory; Henke, 2010). For example, when people experience and later remember an event such as a birthday party or a job interview, they encode multiple, interrelated sets of associations between stimuli and memes (e.g. relating to the people who were present; the series of sub-events in that overall episode; or the places or objects involved). Subsequently, stimuli can potentially evoke a memory of either the entire episode (as a meme or interrelated set of memes) or one or more subcomponents of the episode (as more specific memes). For our purposes, we consider these different forms of memory encoding to effectively have the same result: associations between stimuli and memes.

Because most associations are the product of learning and/or experience, they will not all be equally strong or robust. Generally, the more times an association has been reinforced through repetition (via life experience), the stronger it will be. Associations that have been made once or reinforced only occasionally will not be as strong; over time, associations that are not reinforced may atrophy or ultimately be extinguished.

People's experiences also shape the nature of the associations they have between different memes. For example, someone might associate "chocolate chip cookies" with "grandma" (who baked them) and with "chewy" (a quality of grandma's cookies) via the experiences of eating grandma's chewy cookies. That people form such associations is the foundation of contemporary models of learning and encoding in memory (e.g. Henke, 2010; Rudmann, 2018). Because these associations are learned, and learning is a product of experience, it follows that associations between stimuli and memes, as well as between different memes, can and do vary from person to person. While sets of associations are often shared or similar between people—and particularly so for people from similar backgrounds—they are not universal.

In contemporary models of memory, recall consists of accessing a stored meme when prompted by a stimulus (i.e. an associated sensory cue) (e.g. Henke, 2010). Thus, one way that stimuli can activate meme states is via these direct, learned associations, with stimuli acting as a sensory cue. As discussed above, the strength of these associations varies as a function of previous experience (e.g. repetition). When associations are well-established, this recall can happen rapidly, and require little to no conscious effort. Hearing the word "dog", for example, can rapidly and effortlessly activate the concept of a furry animal that people often have as a pet, along with various associations one might have with it. This is what most people experience with familiar stimuli that are not social in nature. This can also be what people experience when stimuli are part of well-established conventional communicative systems (i.e. "codes"; see Chapter 7), and are used in ways fully consistent with those systems. As discussed in Chapter 1, "code model" explanations of communication essentially rely on the use of such systems.

Preliminary Inference-Making in Context

Most social and/or communicative situations involve social stimuli that are not necessarily used in literal or fully conventional ways, however (e.g. implicature; Grice, 1975, 1989). In these cases, communicators need to make inferences. In explaining how "ambiguous" stimuli (i.e. stimuli with the potential to activate several different meme states) activate a particular meme state, we take as axiomatic that stimuli are always processed in context (e.g. Piantadosi et al., 2012). In other words, people process any given social or communicative stimulus along with other stimuli in the physical and social situation at hand; people do not process stimuli in isolation. As discussed in the previous chapter, we also assume that human cognitive processes are guided by a predisposition toward efficiency (Chapter 3: Premise 2), and we consider prediction to be a core mechanism in human cognition (Chapter 3: Premise 3). Given these assumptions, we propose that stimuli ultimately activate meme states as a joint function of (a) their accessibility, and (b) their fit with predictions generated by communicators' situation models.

As just noted, all communication occurs in context. The physical environment of any given interaction is comprised of stimuli, which may or may not be social in nature. Communicators' interactional history (i.e. what has been said or enacted leading up to the present moment, in this interaction or previous interactions), as well as immediate social situation, also offer stimuli that contribute to an interaction's context. These contextual stimuli serve at least two important functions. First, they contribute to the construction of communicators' initial situation models for an interaction. Second, they can prime the activation of particular meme states in that interaction.

Once a communicative episode is initiated, we propose that communicators immediately construct a tentative situation model of the interaction. The content and nature of this initial, tentative situation model is largely based on contextual stimuli. Among other things, contextual stimuli can activate schemata linked to a physical location or social situation (e.g. "this is a discussion with my neighbor on our street" or "this is a customer service interaction at a store"); they can also circumscribe or narrow the possible purposes or content of an interaction (e.g. "because this is an interaction with a student during office hours, it will likely address class-related topics, and not our hobbies").

In addition to informing the construction of initial situation models, contextual stimuli themselves can activate meme states (e.g. via established associations in memory, as described above). Once a meme state has been activated, it remains more readily accessible for a period of time relative to meme states that have not been recently activated (Pickering & Garrod, 2004; Sharwood Smith, 2019). Additionally, related or associated meme states (i.e. those that have been frequently co-activated in the past) should also be more readily accessible (e.g. Pickering & Garrod, 2004). In this way, contextual stimuli can prime the activation of particular meme states.

In a similar manner, communicators' active situation models can also prime the activation of certain meme states. Situation models incorporate communicators' goals for the interaction, as well as their best estimation of the content of the interaction at a given moment in time, represented as meme states and the structural relationships between them (see Chapter 2). Thus, situation models involve active meme states; as just described, these can prime the activation of related meme states. Additionally, as described in Chapter 2, we conceptualize situation models as both descriptive and predictive. As such, communicators' situation models at a given point in time also offer predictions for what meme state(s) are likely to be activated next. We suggest that these predictions may also prime meme states, so they will require less processing effort to activate, compared to other (not predicted) meme states. (Such priming may also contribute to, and help explain, confirmation bias; Hernandez & Preston, 2013). In short, in a communicative interaction, contextual stimuli and the content of communicators' active situation models prime the activation of particular meme states.

Once communicators start ostensively presenting social stimuli to one another (e.g. speaking, gesturing, making facial expressions), we propose that those stimuli initially activate the meme states that are most accessible, given what is already active. Here, we define accessibility in terms of processing effort: the less processing effort required to activate a meme state, the more accessible that meme state is. Thus, we propose that the meme states that stimuli initially (immediately) activate are those that require the least processing effort, in context. Assuming the stimuli communicators present are not completely literal and explicit (i.e. there is not a one-to-one association between the stimulus presented and a meme in memory), this process of meme state activation can be seen as inference-making.

For example, if two neighbors in the United States were discussing how "the virus" has affected the social dynamics of their neighborhood in the midst of the 2020 Covid-19 (coronavirus) pandemic, use of that term will most likely activate (i.e. lead to the inference) that the speaker is referring to the coronavirus that causes Covid-19, rather than any other virus (e.g. SARS, MERS, H1N1, or an influenza virus). This is because both communicators' situation models will address the pandemic they are currently experiencing and its effects, and these models will predict that subsequent utterances will also relate to this topic. Additionally, features of the interactional context (e.g. wearing face coverings or standing several feet apart while having this conversation) will also likely activate meme states related to Covid-19. Both these factors would make the meme state of "coronavirus that causes Covid-19" more readily accessible than the meme state of "SARS", "MERS" or "influenza". However, if the conversation occurred in Singapore in 2003, the meme state of "SARS" would likely be the most readily accessible meme state for communicators (and therefore the inference that those communicators would expect, and make).

Comparison and Revision

Once an initial meme state is activated (as determined by accessibility) in context, we propose that communicators compare this meme state to the meme state(s) predicted by their situation model. Via this comparison, communicators essentially check whether the meme state that was activated—that is, their inference—is consistent with their current mental model of the nature and content of the interaction. If the content of the newly activated meme state is congruent with the predictions of communicators current situation models, then communicators experience the meme state as "fitting" their model, in context. For instance, if two academic colleagues see each other in the hall and one initiates an interaction with, "How was your class?", that communicator's situation model might represent their conversation as a discussion about his colleague's introductory-level, mass lecture course. Given this, he might predict that his colleague will respond with a comment that addresses her experiences giving a conventional instructional lecture. If the other communicator says, "Class was good; I covered communication competence today" this might activate a meme state in which the colleague delivered a lecture on the topic of communication competence. This meme state would be congruent with the first colleague's predictions, and so would be accepted as "making sense" or "fitting" in context.

However, if the meme state that is initially activated by a given set of stimuli is not consistent with a situation model's prediction, or does not cohere with a situation model more generally, then communicators experience that meme state as not "fitting"; if they are conscious of the discrepancy, they may label the unexpected meme state as "not making sense." For instance, in the example just described, one communicator predicted that his colleague's response would address delivering a lecture. If the other communicator's next remark was, "Class was good; my students were really talkative today", this might activate a meme state in which students were talking a lot in the colleague's class, and the colleague was pleased about that. This meme state would be inconsistent with the first communicator's predictions (because students typically do not talk during a conventional mass lecture class, and if they do, it is generally disruptive rather than desirable). When an inconsistency between a prediction and an activated meme state occurs, we propose that communicators experience arousal (as when an expectancy is violated; Burgoon, 1993; see also Wlotko & Federmeier, 2012). This state of arousal prompts communicators to address the discrepancy between the meme state that was most readily accessible to them in context and their situation models' predictions, which requires additional effort.

Communicators can address such discrepancies in at least three different ways. First, people can search for other possible meme states a given set of stimuli could conceivably activate. Similar to relevance theory (Sperber & Wilson, 1995), we propose that people will essentially iterate, going through the cycle described above repeatedly (each time activating the meme state that is most accessible of the remaining possible options), until a meme state is reached that does fit, or make sense, in the context of their current situation model. For instance, the first communicator might consider the possibility that his colleauge's characterization of her talkative class as "good" was intended as a joke or ironic remark, rather than a sincere one. Concluding that his colleague's comment was, in fact, ironic would activate a meme state consistent with his situation model's prediction, and the discrepancy would be resolved.

As a second strategy, people can reformulate their situation model in a way that allows the (previously) unexpected meme state to make sense in context (Friston, 2010). For instance, the first communicator might adjust his situation model to allow a mass lecture course to involve other activities besides an instructor delivering a lecture. If this expanded model includes possible situations in which an instructor wants students to be talkative (e.g. as students engage in a problem-solving activity in groups), then the discrepancy could be resolved.

As a third strategy, communicators can seek out additional stimuli, and then re-engage in the processes we have just described, with a different set of stimuli as a starting point. For instance, the first communicator might ask for clarification or elaboration ("Talkative? During your mass lecture?"), and use the stimuli his interlocutor presents in response to that question as a basis for meme state activation.

We propose that people will pursue the strategy that is the least effortful, of these options, until they reach an acceptable solution. Such solutions can be pursued either internally or interactively (we address these options in greater detail in Chapter 6). When an acceptable solution is reached, people should no longer experience arousal, and the process of meme state activation is complete. We view this overall process of meme state activation as essentially governed by efficiency (Chapter 3: Premise 2): activating the meme state that is most readily available and only devoting more effort to the process if this initial solution is not sufficient should minimize unnecessary energy expenditure in the meme activation process.

Consequences for Situation Models

Once a satisfactory meme state is activated, we propose that communicators either confirm or update their current situation models accordingly. If that satisfactory meme state is congruent with their situation models' predictions, communicators assimilate the new information into their current model, and essentially confirm that model in terms of its overall structure and content. If arriving at a satisfactory meme state required revising or altering their previous situation models, then the model is updated to reflect the changes necessary for satisfactory meme state activation.

In addition to optimizing the amount of energy used to activate meme states that "make sense" in context, the process we propose here also optimizes the processing effort people engage to construct an accurate situation model of the interaction. (Alternatively stated, this process optimizes the amount of processing effort people use to address prediction error[1] in situation models). As discussed in Chapter 2, we propose that the function of a situation model is to accurately reflect the state, content, and nature of the communicative episode. When a communicator's current situation model is relatively accurate (i.e. prediction error is low), meme state activation entails relatively little processing effort. That communicator also experiences a relatively small magnitude of change (if any) in her situation model as an outcome of the meme activation process. When a communicator's current situation model is not accurate (i.e. prediction error is high), meme state activation entails more processing effort. Once incongruities are resolved—by either activating an alternative meme state, and then updating the situation model accordingly, or updating the situation model directly to accommodate the meme state initially activated—the corresponding magnitude of change (correction) in a communicator's situation model, as an outcome of the meme activation process, is greater. Thus, the amount of processing effort engaged to produce or maintain an accurate situation model is calibrated to the degree of error communicators experience.

The overall process we have described is generally consistent with other theoretical frameworks addressing inferences, such as work on social categorization (e.g. self-categorization theory; Turner et al., 1987). Social categories can be seen as meme states, which communicators infer on the basis of social stimuli. Additionally, and accordingly, a social category (e.g. gender, ethnicity, religious affiliation, etc.) and its associated stereotypes can comprise part of a situation model, and be used to explain and predict what is happening in a communicative episode (Dragojevic & Giles, 2014; Turner et al., 1987). In self-categorization theory, categorization (i.e. which social categories are activated in a given situation) is theorized as a function of *accessibility* and *fit*. *Accessibility* refers to how easily a person can access a given category, and is thus akin to processing effort in our model. *Fit*[2] refers to how well those categories explain the set of characteristics a person is presented with, in context. Thus, fit corresponds to the extent of the discrepancy between the meme state that was most accessible to communicators and their situation model's prediction—that is, the degree of prediction error that communicators experience. Low prediction error (i.e. minimal discrepancy) corresponds to good fit, in self-categorization theory's terms, and vice versa.

The process of meme state activation we have described is also generally consistent with relevance theory's assertions about inference-making (Sperber &

Wilson, 1995). As outlined above, relevance theory's cognitive principle argues the social stimuli that communicators perceive activate the meme state that optimizes the trade-off between processing effort and positive cognitive effects. The process we have outlined leads to this outcome: by engaging only as much energy as is needed to address prediction error, communicators optimize the amount of processing effort used for a given magnitude of change in to their situation model (which corresponds to relevance theory's *positive cognitive effects*, conceptualized as change in mental representations). However, our description provides additional detail on how this potentially occurs. We also offer a novel perspective on the potential mechanisms by which these two considerations are optimized, in a way that is consistent with the Bayesian brain hypothesis, and with a predictive coding framework more generally (e.g. Shamay-Tsoory et al., 2019).

Subjective Experiences of Meme State Activation

Having described the process of meme state activation in cognitive terms, we now briefly address how people subjectively experience this process. When stimuli in context quickly and easily active a meme state that is consistent with their situation model's predictions, people often have little to no awareness of the meme activation process; it is transparent to them. They simply experience "meaning", and feel confident in what the stimuli they processed "mean". Subjectively, people often experience and label such stimuli as "clear" or "straightforward".

When stimuli do not activate a meme state that is consistent with their situation model's prediction, however, people often become more aware of the meme activation process. If stimuli are sufficiently familiar, people may consciously weigh or consider different possible meme states that stimuli in context could potentially activate (e.g. "perhaps he meant his neighbor Sally, rather than our colleague Sally"). They might also consciously consider different (re)formulations of their situation model (e.g. "perhaps he is asking for help, or seeking social support, rather than just telling me about this problem"). In these situations, communicators experience uncertainty about what the stimuli "mean". Subjectively, people often experience and label such stimuli as "confusing", "vague", or "ambiguous".

If stimuli are unfamiliar and/or contextual information is limited, the meme states that those stimuli activate may be at a higher level of abstraction than communicators need to "make sense" of a situation by their usual standards. For example, if someone who is not fluent in Japanese hears a person speaking Japanese, these auditory stimuli might activate "[sounds like] Japanese" instead of the memes associated with particular Japanese words. In situations like these, people tend to experience uncertainty about what stimuli "mean", as they do when stimuli could activate multiple possible meme states. However, this uncertainty may also be accompanied by some degree of awareness that their lack of familiarity with the stimuli is a likely reason for the difficulties they are experiencing.

Summary

In this chapter, we have offered explanations of three key components of social interaction: how people initiate interactions; how (implicitly) consenting to interact shapes subsequent cognition and action; and how stimuli activate specific meme states in communicators' minds. As we have conceptualized understanding as a state of entrainment in communicators' situation models *as a result of at least one person's use of social stimuli*, social interaction is directly implicated in explaining how people create understanding. In line with this, the components of communicating we have presented here will serve as the building blocks for our model of creating understanding, which we present in the next chapter.

Notes

1. Friston (2010), among others, has noted that prediction error can basically be conceptualized as uncertainty, in an information theoretic sense. Viewed this way, the overall process we describe essentially optimizes the trade-off between processing effort and reduction in uncertainty about the content and/or nature of an interaction.
2. Self-categorization describes two types of fit: *normative fit*, the extent to which characteristics are consistent with stereotypes or normative expectations for a given category, and *comparative fit*, the extent to which a category makes sense of similarities and differences in characteristics among comparable entities in context (Turner et al., 1987).

References

Apperly, I. (2018). Mindreading and psycholinguistic approaches to perspective taking: Establishing common ground. *Topics in Cognitive Science, 10*(1), 133–139. https://doi.org/10.1111/tops.12308

Apperly, I. A., & Butterfill, S. A. (2009). Do humans have two systems to track beliefs and belief-like states? *Psychological Review, 116*(4), 953–970. https://doi.org/10.1037/a0016923

Aune, R. K., Levine, T. R., Park, H. S., Asada, K. J. K., & Banas, J. A. (2005). Tests of a theory of communicative responsibility. *Journal of Language and Social Psychology, 24*(4), 358–381. https://doi.org/10.1177/0261927X05281425

Burgoon, J. K. (1993). Interpersonal expectations, expectancy violations, and emotional communication. *Journal of Language and Social Psychology, 12*, 30–48. https://doi.org/10.117 7/0261927X93121003

Ciaramidaro, A., Becchio, C., Colle, L., Bara, B. G., & Walter, H. (2014). Do you mean me? Communicative intentions recruit the mirror and the mentalizing system. *Social Cognitive and Affective Neuroscience, 9*(7), 909–916. https://doi.org/10.1093/scan/nst062

Clark, H. H. (1996). *Using language.* Cambridge University Press. https://doi.org/10.1017/ CBO9780511620539

Dragojevic, M., & Giles, H. (2014). The reference frame effect: An intergroup perspective on language attitudes. *Human Communication Research, 40*(1), 91–111. https://doi. org/10.1111/hcre.12017

Friston, K. (2010). The free-energy principle: A unified brain theory?. *Nature Reviews Neuroscience, 11*(2), 127–138. https://doi.org/10.1038/nrn2787

Frith, C. D., & Frith, U. (2005). Theory of mind. *Current Biology, 15*(17), R644-R645. https:// doi.org/10.1016/j.cub.2005.08.041

Grice, H. P. (1975). Logic and conversation. In P. Cole & J. Morgan (Eds.), *Syntax and semantics* (Vol. 3, pp. 41–58). Academic Press.

Grice, H. P. (1989). *Studies in the way of words.* Harvard University Press.

Hassin, R. R., Aarts, H., & Ferguson, M. J. (2005). Automatic goal inferences. *Journal of Experimental Social Psychology, 41*, 129–140. https://doi.org/10.1016/j.jesp.2004.06.008

Heider, F. (1958/2013). *The psychology of interpersonal relations.* Psychology Press.

Heider, F., & Simmel, M. (1944). An experimental study of apparent behavior. *The American Journal of Psychology, 57*(2), 243–259. https://doi.org/10.2307/1416950

Henke, K. (2010). A model for memory systems based on processing modes rather than consciousness. *Nature Reviews Neuroscience, 11*(7), 523–532. https://doi.org/10.1038/nrn2850

Hernandez, I., & Preston, J. L. (2013). Disfluency disrupts the confirmation bias. *Journal of Experimental Social Psychology, 49*(1), 178–182. https://doi.org/10.1016/j.jesp.2012.08.010

Levine, T. R. (2014). Truth-default theory (TDT): A theory of human deception and deception detection. *Journal of Language and Social Psychology, 33*(4), 378–392. https://doi.org/ 10.1177/0261927X14535916

Levinson, S. C. (2006). On the human "interaction engine". In N. J. Enfield & S. C. Levinson (Eds.), *Roots of human sociality: Culture, cognition, and interaction* (pp. 39–69). Berg.

Malle, B. F., & Holbrook, J. (2012). Is there a hierarchy of social inferences? The likelihood and speed of inferring intentionality, mind, and personality. *Journal of Personality and Social Psychology, 102*, 661–684. https://doi.org/10.1037/a0026790

O'Grady, C., Kliesch, C., Smith, K., & Scott-Phillips, T. (2015). The ease and extent of recursive mindreading, across implicit and explicit tasks. *Evolution and Human Behavior, 36*(4), 313–322. https://doi.org/10.1016/j.evolhumbehav.2015.01.004

Piantadosi, S. T., Tily, H., & Gibson, E. (2012). The communicative function of ambiguity in language. *Cognition, 122*(3), 280–291. https://doi.org/10.1016/j.cognition.2011.10.004

Pickering, M. J., & Garrod, S. (2004). Toward a mechanistic psychology of dialogue. *Behavioral and Brain Sciences, 27*(2), 169–190. https://doi.org/10.1017/S0140525X04000056

Rudmann, D. (2018). *Learning and memory.* SAGE.

Schneider, D., Slaughter, V. P., & Dux, P. E. (2015). What do we know about implicit false-belief tracking?. *Psychonomic Bulletin & Review, 22*(1), 1–12. https://doi.org/10.3758/s13423-014-0644-z

Scott-Phillips, T. C. (2015). *Speaking our minds: Why human communication is different, and how language evolved to make it special.* Palgrave Macmillan.

Shamay-Tsoory, S. G., Saporta, N., Marton-Alper, I. Z., & Gvirts, H. Z. (2019). Herding brains: A core neural mechanism for social alignment. *Trends in Cognitive Sciences, 23*(3), 174–186. https://doi.org/10.1016/j.tics.2019.01.002

Sharwood Smith, M. (2019). The compatibility within a modular framework of emergent and dynamical processes in mind and brain. *Journal of Neurolinguistics, 49*, 240–244. https://doi.org/10.1016/j.jneuroling.2018.04.010

Shulman, H. C., Dixon, G. N., Bullock, O. M., & Colón Amill, D. (2020). The effects of jargon on processing fluency, self-perceptions, and scientific engagement. *Journal of Language and Social Psychology.* https://doi.org/10.1177/0261927X20902177

Sillars, A. L. (1998). (Mis)Understanding. In B. H. Spitzberg & W. R. Cupach (Eds.), *The dark side of personal relationships* (pp. 73–102). Erlbaum.

Smith, E., & Miller, F. (1983). Mediation among attributional inferences and comprehension processes: Initial findings and a general method. *Journal of Personality and Social Psychology, 44*, 492–505. https://doi.org/10.1037/0022-3514.44.3.492

Sperber, D., & Wilson, D. (1995). *Relevance: Communication and cognition (2nd Ed.).* Blackwell.

Turner, J. C., Hogg, M. A., Oakes, P. J., Reicher, S. D. & Wetherell, M. S. (1987). A self-categorization theory. *Rediscovering the social group: A self-categorization theory* (pp. 42–66). Basil Blackwell.

Wlotko, E. W., & Federmeier, K. D. (2012). So that's what you meant! Event-related potentials reveal multiple aspects of context use during construction of message-level meaning. *NeuroImage, 62*(1), 356–366. https://doi.org/10.1016/j.neuroimage.2012.04.054

CHAPTER FIVE

Creating Understanding

This chapter outlines a process model of how people create understanding. We propose that when people communicate ostensively, they present social stimuli that activate meme states. They also construct, test, and refine situation models of a social interaction on the basis of these meme states. More specifically, we propose that people go through an iterative process of (a) comparing predictions generated by their situation models to the meme states that are most accessible to them in context, and (b) confirming or revising the content of their situation model to address prediction errors. By continuously updating their situation models to minimize prediction error in a shared experience (i.e. an interaction), communicators' situation models become entrained. When communicators successfully entrain their situation models, they create a state of understanding.

Summarizing and drawing together our foundational assumptions (Chapter 2), observations about human behavior and cognition (Chapter 3), and the components of communicating (Chapter 4) proposed in the previous chapters, we now outline our process model of how people create understanding. In what follows, our description is written in a manner that presumes that communicators share a goal of creating understanding—that is, of entraining situation models, and their associated meme states. We do recognize that this is not always the case, and that understanding is not always communicators' primary goal in interaction; we discuss such situations in greater detail in the next chapter. However, we contend that even when a communicator wishes to derail, subvert, or manipulate understanding, the process we will describe is still the backbone of the corresponding social interaction. In what follows, we present our model of this process, and briefly outline some its implications for understanding. We then discuss how this model addresses problems that people experience with understanding (i.e. "misunderstanding"), and conclude with a discussion of the role of implicit versus explicit cognition in the proposed model.

Creating Understanding: A Process Model

We begin with initiating interaction. When people want to communicate, they present stimuli (e.g. vocalizing, a gesture, eye contact) as an indication of that desire. Because people do not have direct access to others' minds, they must use stimuli—which are accessible to other people—as evidence of their intentions. This is possible because people assume that mental states are the basis for each other's behavior, and treat stimuli from their interlocutors as being indicative of interlocutors' mental states. This approach to social stimuli is a product of humans' social orientation (Chapter 3: Premise 1). Once stimuli are recognized as evidence of a communicative intention, an ostensive communicative episode is initiated. Following this, communicators implicitly presume that they share a goal of creating understanding, attend to the stimuli that their interaction partners present, and attend to each other's knowledge and beliefs.

Once a communicative episode is initiated, communicators also spontaneously construct tentative situation models for the interaction. Each communicators' initial situation model is largely based on contextual input (which can include physical and social context in general terms, as well as the interpersonal and interactional history of the people involved), and is informed by their own intentions and goals for interaction (Dragojevic et al., 2016). This initial situation model consists of each communicator's best guess at what the communicative episode is or will be about. In line with this, the situation model also offers predictions for what will happen next in the interaction. Following Pickering and Garrod (2013), we propose this predictive modeling occurs on multiple, connected levels: people in interaction make predictions about what meme states are likely to be activated next (which corresponds to the content of the interaction), as well as what stimuli (e.g. words, gestures, etc.) are likely to be used to do so (e.g. Stephens et al., 2010). This predictive modeling also encompasses both production and processing—that is, people model what their interlocutor is likely to activate and/or do next, as well as what they (themselves) will activate and/or do next (Pickering & Garrod, 2013). Generally, these predictive processes should enhance the speed and fluidity of interaction—for example, contributing to rapid, near-seamless turn-taking in conversation (Levinson, 2006).

With the initial situation models that communicators have constructed in mind, communicators present stimuli to each other. More specifically, they present stimuli with the aim of activating meme states in each other's minds that correspond to their own informative intentions. Communicators select stimuli that they believe are optimally relevant for their interlocutors, and expect that the stimuli their interlocutors provide are (optimally) relevant for them, in context (Sperber & Wilson, 1995). These stimuli initially activate the meme state that requires the least effort for a given communicator (who is processing those stimuli) to access. Both contextual stimuli and the content of communicators' situation models play an important role in this process by rendering some meme states more accessible than others.

Once an initial meme state is activated, communicators compare that meme state to the prediction offered by their situation models. When the activated meme state and their predictions approximately match, communicators assimilate the specifics of the newly activated meme state into their current model. In so doing, they essentially confirm that situation model. When the activated meme state and their predictions do not match (which can occur to varying degrees), communicators engage more processing effort to address the discrepancy. To reduce or eliminate the discrepancy, they can (a) search for an alternative meme state (iteratively activating the next-most-accessible option, until something satisfactory is found); (b) modify their situation model to account for the previously unexpected meme state (Friston & Frith, 2015; Pickering & Garrod, 2013); or (c) seek out additional stimuli and begin the comparison process again. Once communicators reach an acceptable solution (generally, by engaging the strategy or strategies, in sequence, that requires the least effort), they revise their situation model accordingly. In this way, situation models are continuously confirmed and/or updated.

In interaction, both communicators engage in these activities (i.e. predicting, processing stimuli, experiencing meme activation, comparing meme states to predictions, updating situation models) simultaneously, and more or less continuously. As noted earlier, the function of a situation model is to accurately represent the state, content, and nature of the communicative episode. The process of revising situation models to minimize prediction error should progressively increase the accuracy of communicators' situation models as representations of the unfolding interaction. Because communicative episodes are joint endeavors, an accurate situation model must account for the behavior, and by extension cognition, of all parties involved—that is, a situation model should capture what one's interlocutors are doing and thinking. Thus, each communicator pursues a model that accurately represents what all other communicators are thinking and doing (which is, in turn, represented in those communicators' own models). If all communicators do so successfully, the result should be a convergence, or alignment, of situation models: entrainment (Friston & Frith, 2015b). This is a state of *understanding*: as described in Chapter 2, communicators successfully create a state of understanding when their situation models are entrained to the extent required for their purposes.

Implications for Understanding

The process we have proposed has a number of potential implications for theorizing about human communication. Here, we wish to highlight three implications of our model that relate specifically to the construct of understanding; we will discuss its implications for communication more generally in the final two chapters of this book.

One implication of the process model we have proposed is that understanding is a state that minimizes prediction error in communicators' mental models. As situation models are not only descriptive but also predictive, communicators who share the same situation model for a communicative episode should both represent *and predict* each other's meme states with a reasonable degree of accuracy. In other words, communicators who have created a state of understanding should be able to accurately predict what their interlocutors will do, and activate, next; accurate predictions entail minimal prediction error (by definition). In line with this, Friston and Frith (2015a) have argued that when two agents share the same generative model for mental predictions at the neurological level, they should experience synchronization of (mental) systems, which should minimize prediction errors (p. 130). In the context of human communication, we propose that a conceptual analogue for their "generative model" could be the situation model for a communicative episode.

Closely related, a second implication of our model is that understanding is a state that optimizes energy use by communicators. We have proposed that inconsistencies between predictions and meme state activation require additional effort to address (i.e. by requiring additional cycles of considering alternative meme states or potential reformulations of a working situation model). Sharing the same "working model" of an interaction—that is, entraining situation models—should also allow interactants to minimize prediction error, as just described above. It follows that minimizing prediction error (as in a state of understanding) should also correspond to minimizing the amount of effort used to arrive at a given meme state, and an accurate situation model, in interaction. Thus, a state of understanding (i.e. entrained situation models) should optimize energy use in the process of communicating (Chapter 3: Premise 2).

Finally, a third implication of our model is that understanding is dynamic. As we have proposed it, the "engine" driving the (potential) entrainment of situation models is meme state activation. Through the process of predicting what meme state will be activated next, testing the most accessible meme state against that prediction, and updating situation models to address prediction errors, situation models can and do change over the course of an interaction. This process is what enables initially disparate situation models to ultimately entrain, or converge, as a result of communicators presenting stimuli that activate meme states. However, entrainment or alignment is not an inevitable outcome of this process; it only occurs if and when communicators are successful in accurately modeling their shared interaction. Each time new stimuli are presented, the cycle of meme state activation begins anew, and there is an opportunity to improve, sustain, or diminish the degree of entrainment communicators are currently experiencing. Thus, entrainment of situation models is a transitory state that has to be constantly readdressed as new stimuli and corresponding meme states are introduced.

Degrees of Understanding

In the way we have described the process of creating understanding, we recognize that it may sound as if understanding is a categorical product—that is, it is something that is achieved or not achieved. At this juncture, we would like to take a moment to address this point. We want to emphasize that we do not conceptualize understanding as a categorical outcome; rather, we view understanding—and thus, entrainment of situation models—as occurring to various degrees in different situations.

Because situation models are multidimensional, they address a range of different facets of an interaction. Each of these facets, particularly those relating to content, can also be rendered in varying levels of detail. Thus, it is possible that communicators may align on some dimensions of a situation model while remaining partially or wholly misaligned on others. For instance, communicators may entrain with respect to semantic content (e.g. understanding that a speaker's cup is empty, following the statement, "My cup is empty") but misalign on the pragmatic nature of the statement (e.g. the speaker may intend this as an observation, while his interlocutor may interpret it as a request to refill the cup). Similarly, communicators may entrain on a social or relational dimension of a situation model (e.g. understanding that one communicator is excluding another from his social group) even when they are not aligned on semantic content (e.g. because one communicator is speaking a language that the other does not know). As a final example, communicators may entrain their situation models with respect to semantic content only up to a particular level of detail (e.g. as when a student who is new to a topic understands the basics of a concept taught by a professor, but not all the details the professor's mental model includes). Thus, in objective terms, we can think of understanding as having degrees in terms of these different dimensions and levels of detail, with a high degree of understanding occurring when most (to all) dimensions of a situation model are entrained.

As we discussed in Chapter 2, we consider communicators to have successfully created understanding when their situation models are sufficiently congruent *for their present purposes*. Communicators come to an interaction with goals, and these goals delineate the "present purposes" that define understanding for those communicators, in context. Thus, we think of understanding as having degrees in terms of the extent to which the entrainment that communicators experience is sufficient for their purposes. With that said, communicators may subjectively experience understanding as a dichotomy, defined by the threshold of entrainment needed to accomplish their goals. When the entrainment that communicators (believe they) experience is sufficient for their needs, those communicators will think that they have understood each other, even if there is a substantial lack of entrainment on some dimensions of their situation models. Likewise, when the entrainment communicators (believe they experience) is not sufficient for their needs, they will think that they have not understood each other, even if there is substantial entrainment on many dimensions of their situation models. In this latter case, people typically label their experience as "misunderstanding" or "miscommunication."

There are several different ways in which a lack of sufficient entrainment can subjectively manifest. Insufficient entrainment can occur intentionally or unintentionally (depending on communicators' goals); in what follows, we focus on the descriptive nature of different possibilities, rather than the range of goals that could motivate them. Because both meme states and situation models are internal and accessible only to their owners, communicators never truly know whether their mental representations are, in fact, successfully entrained in the manner they intend or desire. We propose that people generally manage this by presuming the process is successful until they have evidence to the contrary (e.g. Clark & Brennan, 1991).

When people experience subjectively unproblematic meme state activation—with the meme states activated being largely consistent with their situation model's predictions—communicators proceed with the assumption that they are successfully creating understanding. In this case, it is possible that communicators could experience a state where they both believe that understanding has been created, but be incorrect in that assessment. In this, neither communicator may realize there are important (for their purposes) differences in their active meme states and/or situation models. For example, two people could agree to meet at a chain coffee shop with multiple locations, and believe they are agreeing to meet at the same place while each actually has a different location in mind. (This lack of sufficient entrainment is likely to be recognized when their meeting time arrives, and they find themselves in different places). This situation can be thought of as a "false positive" for understanding.

It is also possible that one or both communicators could realize they have disparate situation models activated. This may occur when stimuli activate meme states that cannot be readily integrated into communicators' working situation models. (It should be noted that communicators can transition from one of these states to another; for instance, they may initially not realize that their situation models are not entrained, but become aware of it as the interaction progresses). For example, in a conversation between colleagues, one or both people may realize that their mental models of an approach to solving a technical problem are not aligned. In this case, communicators still experience misunderstanding, but their awareness creates an opportunity for repair (which can occur either internally or interactively, as described above). Whether people actually engage in that repair depends on a number of factors; we discuss this in greater detail in the next chapter.

Finally, it is also possible for communicators to experience a "false negative" for understanding—that is, communicators can experience a state in in which their situation models are entrained in the way they intend, but they do not realize it. In this case, communicators may either (incorrectly) believe they have disparate situation models activated, or they may also be (consciously) oblivious to the issue of understanding, and any related assessments. For example, an instructor may look at his students' faces and think that they have not constructed accurate situation models of the day's lecture content, when in fact many students have. (It is also possible an instructor could fail to think about whether or not he is successfully creating understanding with his students at all, though we hope this is not the case). From this "false negative" situation, two possible outcomes could follow. First, one or more communicators could end their interaction with a false perception that misunderstanding has occurred. Second, the communicators could continue communicating until they discover that, in fact, they have successfully created understanding.

Implicit and Explicit Mental Representations

We conclude this chapter with a note on the role of explicit versus implicit mental representations, and processing more generally, in the model we have outlined. The extent to which communication actually involves or requires explicitly representing others' mental states or perspectives (i.e. explicit mentalizing) has been a topic of scholarly debate (e.g. Apperly, 2018; Heyes, 2014; Pickering & Garrod, 2004; Shintel & Keysar, 2009). In describing cognitive processes, as we have above, it can often sound as if any part of a process that is explicitly laid out must itself be explicit, conscious, or effortful in nature. Similarly, in explicitly describing the kinds of mental representations required for ostensive-inferential communication (i.e. communication in which interlocutors make manifest their intentions to communicate something specific; Sperber & Wilson, 1995), it can sound as if communicators' intentions and inferences about others' mental states or intentions must also be explicit.

For this reason, we wish to emphasize that in the model we have proposed, we do not see stimuli selection, meme state activation, or entrainment as inherently explicit or effortful sub-processes. They *can* be effortful or consciously controlled, under particular circumstances, but they are not necessarily so. Indeed, we contend that they are often subconscious and minimally effortful. Because the processes of both meme state activation and entrainment are governed by a basic human drive for efficiency (Chapter 3: Premise 2), the manner in which they are undertaken should optimize energy use. Explicit processing is resource-intensive, so we would expect it to only be used when the situation requires it—that is, when other, less resource-intensive options have failed to produce an acceptable outcome.

As we have stated to in our description of this model, one mechanism that can enable and/or facilitate entrainment without significant processing costs is priming. In their *interactive alignment model*, Pickering and Garrod (2004, 2006) argue that priming is actually the main mechanism by which interactants come to align their situation models. We do not necessarily posit that priming is the *main* mechanism through which communicators come to entrain their situation models; however, we do see priming playing an important role in these processes. Specifically, as described above, we contend that once stimuli activate a meme state, this meme state and related meme states—as well as the stimuli used to activate them—are subsequently more easily accessible to both interactants, and that this occurs via priming. Priming results in less processing effort required to (a) access these mental representations, or conceptually related representations, and (b) use that specific set of stimuli for this purpose, at later points in the interactions. This orients people towards these representations when presented with potentially ambiguous stimuli in context. It also facilitates and reinforces the use of particular stimuli to activate specific meme states in an interaction, which helps explain why people tend to converge in their use of stimuli (e.g. words, syntactic structures, gestures) for specific purposes in interaction, which is a well-documented phenomenon (e.g. Dragojevic, et al., 2016; Ireland & Pennebaker, 2010; Pickering & Garrod, 2004). Thus, priming is one means through which communicators can activate meme states and align situation models while engaging minimal mental resources.

We also want to underscore that we do not see explicit mentalizing as a required component of the process of creating understanding. Put another way, it is possible for two (or more) people to successfully entrain their situation models without consciously modeling or representing each other's mental states or perspectives. First, people can experience entrained meme states or situation models as a result of independent engagement of attention and memory in a shared context. As Apperly (2018) observes, "in many cases, the information made available from priming, automatic memory retrieval, and attention cueing track closely enough with the content of a partner's perspective that it can serve the job of coordinating between speakers without the need for perspectives to be represented" (p. 134).

People can also predict mental states or behavior by simulating an experience as their own (e.g. Pickering & Garrod, 2013). People's fundamental social orientation (Chapter 3: Premise 1) underlies this ability, as it enables communicators to recognize (typically, implicitly) that other people have mental experiences that drive behavior, and that these experiences and their outcomes are potentially similar to a communicator's own. If communicators each generate elements of their own situation models via simulation, they can potentially arrive at congruent situation models without having to explicitly think of that model as representing their interlocutor's mental state.

Finally, we consider it possible to engage in spontaneous, implicit mentalizing (e.g. Apperly, 2018; Apperly & Butterfill, 2009; O'Grady et al., 2019; Schneider et al., 2015), which is also enabled by people's social orientation (Chapter 3: Premise 1). Implicit mentalizing should offer content that communicators can draw on during meme state activation (e.g. relating to others' probable knowledge, beliefs, or intentions, which may prime particular meme states). Having communicators' meme state activation informed by this content should facilitate making predictions that are consistent with their interlocutor's situation model—in other words, it should help people more accurately infer what their interlocutors are thinking. In this way, implicit mentalizing should promote the entrainment of situation models, and therefore, understanding.

In all these cases, communicators can create understanding, or take significant steps toward it, without explicit or conscious modeling of another person's mind. With that said, people certainly can and sometimes do explicitly represent what others are thinking. As discussed above, this frequently occurs when implicit processes have not led to sensible or satisfactory outcomes. Thus, we see explicit mentalizing as a possible, but not necessary, component of creating understanding.

Summary

In this chapter, we have outlined a process model of how people create understanding (the limitations of which are addressed in the final chapter of this book). We have proposed that once people initiate an ostensive communicative episode, communicators construct an initial situation model of the interaction based primarily on contextual stimuli. Communicators then present social stimuli that activate meme states. People then engage in cycles of (a) comparing predictions generated by their situation models to the meme states that are most accessible to them in context, and (b) addressing prediction errors by revising the content of their situation model. Through this process of continuously updating their situation models to minimize prediction error in a communicative episode, which is an inherently joint endeavor, communicators' situation models become entrained—that is, communicators create a state of understanding. In the final sections of this chapter, we discussed some implications of this model for theorizing about understanding, and the ways in which a lack of entrainment ("misunderstanding") can be subjectively experienced.

References

Apperly, I. (2018). Mindreading and psycholinguistic approaches to perspective taking: Establishing common ground. *Topics in Cognitive Science*, *10*(1), 133–139. https://doi.org/10.1111/tops.12308

Apperly, I. A., & Butterfill, S. A. (2009). Do humans have two systems to track beliefs and belief-like states? *Psychological Review*, *116*(4), 953–970. https://doi.org/10.1037/a0016923

Clark, H. H., & Brennan, S. E. (1991). Grounding in communication. In L. B. Resnick, J. M. Levine, & S. D. Teasley (Eds.), *Perspectives on socially shared cognition*, (pp. 127–149). American Psychological Association.

Dragojevic, M., Gasiorek, J., & Giles, H. (2016). Accommodative strategies as core of CAT. In H. Giles (Ed.), *Communication accommodation theory: Negotiating personal and social identities across contexts* (pp. 36–59). Cambridge University Press. https://doi.org/10.1017/CBO9781316226537.003

Friston, K. J., & Frith, C. D. (2015a). Active inference, communication and hermeneutics. *Cortex*, *68*, 129–143. https://doi.org/10.1016/j.cortex.2015.03.025

Friston, K. J., & Frith, C. D. (2015b). A duet for one. *Consciousness and Cognition*, *36*, 390–405. https://doi.org/10.1016/j.concog.2014.12.003

Heyes, C. (2014). Submentalizing: I am not really reading your mind. *Perspectives on Psychological Science*, *9*(2), 131–143. https://doi.org/10.1177/1745691613518076

Ireland, M. E., & Pennebaker, J. W. (2010). Language style matching in writing: Synchrony in essays, correspondence, and poetry. *Journal of Personality and Social Psychology*, *99*, 549–571. https://doi.org/10.1037/a0020386

Levinson, S. C. (2006). On the human "interaction engine". In N. J. Enfield & S. C. Levinson (Eds.), *Roots of human sociality: Culture, cognition, and interaction* (pp. 39–69). Berg.

O'Grady, C., Scott-Phillips, T., Lavelle, S., & Smith, K. (2019, March 1). Perspective-taking is spontaneous but not automatic. https://doi.org/10.31219/osf.io/wzcqs

Pickering, M. J., & Garrod, S. (2004). Toward a mechanistic psychology of dialogue. *Behavioral and Brain Sciences*, *27*(2), 169–190. https://doi.org/10.1017/S0140525X04000056

Pickering, M. J., & Garrod, S. (2006). Alignment as the basis for successful communication. *Research on Language and Computation*, *4*(2–3), 203–228. https://doi.org/10.1007/s11168-006-9004-0

Pickering, M. J., & Garrod, S. (2013). An integrated theory of language production and comprehension. *Behavioral and Brain Sciences*, *36*(4), 329–347. https://doi.org/10.1017/S0140525X12001495

Schneider, D., Slaughter, V. P., & Dux, P. E. (2015). What do we know about implicit false-belief tracking? *Psychonomic Bulletin & Review*, *22*(1), 1–12. https://doi.org/10.3758/s13423-014-0644-z

Shintel, H., & Keysar, B. (2009). Less is more: A minimalist account of joint action in communication. *Topics in Cognitive Science*, *1*(2), 260–273. https://doi.org/10.1111/j.1756-8765.2009.01018.x

Sperber, D., & Wilson, D. (1995). *Relevance: Communication and cognition (2nd Ed.)*. Blackwell.

Stephens, G. J., Silbert, L. J., & Hasson, U. (2010). Speaker-listener neural coupling underlies successful communication. *Proceedings of the National Academy of Sciences*, *107*, 14425–14430. https://doi.org/10.1073/pnas.1008662107

CHAPTER SIX

Contextual Factors

In this chapter, we discuss how a subset of contextual factors can affect the process of creating understanding. We first address how the degree of reciprocity and synchrony that an interactional context allows can affect how communicators approach creating understanding, and how they address ambiguities and potential misunderstandings. We then consider the medium of communication as a contextual variable, and discuss how affordances of different communication media can affect the way people create understanding. Next, we address how social and cultural norms can filter stimuli presentation and moderate meme state activation in the process of creating understanding. Finally, we briefly address how communicators' goals can affect the stimuli they select and how situation models are adjusted through interaction.

In the framework we have proposed so far, we have focused on core concepts and processes involved in creating understanding. We consider the model we have outlined in Chapter 5 to be a general process model that applies across contexts. However, there are also many factors not included in our process model that can affect how people engage in the process of creating understanding. We now turn to a discussion of a subset of such contextual factors. In what follows, we first discuss reciprocity and synchrony as features of the interactive context that can influence how people engage in disambiguation and error correction. We then address the role of the medium of communication in creating understanding. Next, we discuss how social and cultural norms can affect subcomponents of the process of creating understanding we have proposed. Lastly, we address how communicators' goals can influence the degree and nature of entrainment of situation models, as well as stimuli selection in interaction. Through this, we hope to offer insight into how situational factors can moderate or otherwise influence the processes we have described in previous chapters, and to provide a fuller picture of how people create understanding in different contexts.

Interactional Context

In the previous chapter, we argued that contextual stimuli play an important role in creating understanding: directly and indirectly, they can prime the activation of specific meme states, making those meme states less effortful to access than others. We now address context at a more macro level: the interactional context. In what follows, we focus on two dimensions that affect how people interact when communicating: the extent to which contexts allow (a) *reciprocity* and *(b) synchrony* in the flow of stimuli.

Reciprocity addresses the direction(s) that stimuli flow (Stromer-Galley, 2004). In some contexts, stimuli readily flow in two or more directions (e.g. having face-to-face or telephone conversations, where each person can readily provide and access vocal and/or visual stimuli). In these situations, communicative reciprocity is high. In other contexts, stimuli primarily flow in one direction (e.g. watching mass media broadcasts or reading a book, where stimuli generally flow from author to audience, but not the reverse). In these situations, communicative reciprocity is low.

Synchrony addresses the time scale of interaction (e.g. Burgoon, Giles, & Dunbar, 2017; Haeckel, 1998). The more synchronous an interaction, the more we see stimuli from different communicators closely follow each other in a coordinated way. Thus, when two things are aligned in time, they are considered relatively *synchronous* with each other. Conversely, when two things are separated in time or uncoordinated in their timing, they are *asynchronous* (with each other). Typically, face-to-face and telephone conversations are examples of synchronous interactive situations, as people speak and respond to each other in real time (or with minimal delays) in highly coordinated ways. In contrast, conversations over email are less synchronous; people can send an email and not get a reply for a day, a week, or even a month (and these delays are not always predictable). Books are almost totally asynchronous: people can, and do, read texts that were written by authors decades or even centuries ago.

Both synchrony and reciprocity affect communicators' opportunities to (a) provide feedback, and (b) modify the stimuli they provide, with implications for creating understanding. In reciprocal contexts, people can readily and easily provide feedback to each other. For instance, they can indicate (through their own use of stimuli) what they believe has been communicated, offering their interlocutor a chance to confirm or deny their inferences. They can also ask questions if they are having difficulty with stimuli in context (e.g. "Sorry, say again?"; "Who is Sally?"). Communicators can also provide confirmations, acknowledgments (e.g. through backchanneling), or contradictions of the feedback offered by their interlocutors (Clark, 1996). However, this is not possible, or the opportunities for it are limited, in contexts with low levels of reciprocity (e.g. Clark & Krych, 2004). For example, people generally provide each other with ongoing feedback throughout face-to-face conversations (a reciprocal interactive context). However, people generally do not provide feedback to media broadcasters whose programming they watch, or book authors whose work they read (as these are typically nonreciprocal contexts).

Generally, the more synchronous the interactional context is, the more readily communicators will engage in feedback as part of the process of creating understanding, all other things being equal (Dennis et al., 2008). It is important to note that synchrony does not strictly affect the *ability* to provide feedback: as long as stimuli can flow bilaterally between communicators, feedback is theoretically possible. However, if there are long delays between the initial presentation of stimuli and feedback (as well as any response to that feedback; see below), it is generally not an efficient way to address problems or issues related to understanding that may arise. As such, in asynchronous interactional contexts, people are less likely to view seeking or providing feedback as useful to the process of creating understanding. For example, as noted above, people readily provide feedback in face-to-face conversations, which are highly synchronous. However, people typically provide less feedback (especially feedback specifically addressing the nature of stimuli presented, as it relates to understanding) over email, which is more asynchronous.

In reciprocal interactive contexts, communicators can also revise or add to the social stimuli they offer in response to the feedback they receive ("I said, 'pass the hot sauce'"; "Sally is a professor in the chemistry department"). As noted in earlier chapters, Clark and Brennan (1991) refer to this interactive process of establishing and confirming intended meaning as *grounding* (i.e. establishing what is *common ground*: mutual knowledge, beliefs, and assumptions; Clark, 1996; Clark & Krych, 2004). When synchrony is high, the process of offering modifications to previously presented stimuli can occur quickly, and in real time; when synchrony is low, this process can be slow and protracted. We propose that people consider these factors when deciding whether to seek or provide additional stimuli in social interactions. All other things being equal, the less reciprocal or synchronous the interactive context, the less likely people are to seek or offer additional stimuli, and/or engage in overt grounding. This is likely because it is either less possible or less efficient (Chapter 3: Premise 2) to do so when reciprocity and/or synchrony is lower, as opposed to higher.

In nonreciprocal contexts (e.g. a pre-recorded speech), people can offer reformulations or modifications of stimuli they have already presented (e.g. restating a point in different words; offering a correction of a previous statement; Garrod et al., 2007). However, because such contexts do not allow people to easily receive feedback, these modifications may or may not address any issues or concerns their fellow communicators (i.e. audience) might have had with the stimuli initially presented. Thus, such modifications may or may not actually facilitate understanding.

Implications: Disambiguation and Error Correction

In the previous chapter, we proposed that when the meme states activated in interaction are generally consistent with the predictions offered by communicators' situation models, those communicators experience interaction as subjectively unproblematic, and they assume they are successfully creating understanding (e.g. Clark & Brennan, 1991). However, if the meme states initially activated in interaction are not consistent with their situation models' predictions, communicators have to resolve this discrepancy. In this situation, communicators experience arousal, which prompts them to take additional steps to engage in disambiguation and/or error correction.

In our process model of creating understanding, we proposed three possible options to address discrepancies between the meme state initially activated and a situation model's prediction. One option is to search for other possible meme states a given set of stimuli could activate. Another option is to reformulate one's situation model in a way that allows the (previously) unexpected meme state to make sense in context. The final option is to seek out additional stimuli, and begin the process of meme state activation anew. We proposed that communicators could pursue these options internally (that is, in the communicator's mind, without outside intervention), or interactively.

In line with humans' predisposition toward efficiency (Chapter 3: Premise 2), we proposed that people will generally pursue the route to an acceptable solution that is least effortful (all other things being equal). If that route does not work, they will repeat their efforts with the next-least effortful route. This should occur in cycles of attempts, with effort escalating in each cycle, until a solution is reached. In general, we expect internal routes (i.e. considering alternative meme states stimuli could activate or adjusting one's situation model on one's own) are likely to require less effort than interactive routes, so they are likely to be pursued first.

If internal attempts at addressing problematic meme state activation are unsuccessful, and interaction is an option, communicators may switch to an interactive approach. Examples of interactive strategies include asking their interlocutor questions about what meme state was intended (e.g. "Do you mean …?"), interrogating aspects of the situation model (e.g. "Are you asking me to close the window?"), or expressing their uncertainty in the hopes of being provided new or modified stimuli to work with (e.g. "I'm not sure what you mean").

Whether interactive disambiguation and/or error correction is possible or likely in a given situation depends at least in part on the degree of reciprocity and synchrony available. Generally, the degree of reciprocity determines whether this is possible. In reciprocal contexts, it is possible to engage in interactive disambiguation (because stimuli flow is bi- or multidirectional between communicators), while in nonreciprocal situations it generally is not (because stimuli flow only in one direction).

The degree of synchrony, as well as the degree of effort required to generate stimuli in a given medium (see below), should predict the likelihood that people will engage in interactive disambiguation or error correction. If the interactive context is highly synchronous and it is relatively easy to ask questions or present stimuli (e.g. as in a face-to-face conversation), communicators are more likely to attempt interactive "solutions" to ambiguous or problematic meme state activation than they are in situations that are less synchronous, and/or where it is more difficult to provide feedback or modify stimuli.

Implications: Stimuli Selection

Reciprocity and synchrony also have implications for communicators' approaches to selecting and presenting stimuli. When stimuli can be easily modified and revised, the initial set of stimuli someone selects does not have to be the only or final version. As a result, presenting stimuli in highly reciprocal and synchronous contexts tends to be more *dynamic*, and interactants may select stimuli more rapidly, accepting that they may later be revised. In such situations, people can employ a rapid, "guess and check" approach to creating understanding. For instance, in face-to-face conversations (which are highly reciprocal and synchronous) people typically construct utterances rapidly, in real time. When they experience stimuli as ambiguous and/or experience inconsistencies between their situation model's predictions and the meme states that stimuli activate, communicators often ask questions to seek clarification (as this is possible to do, and asking questions generally does not require high levels of effort). Their interlocutors, in turn, restate or reformulate the stimuli they provide in response to those queries and requests. In such dynamic situations, stimuli selection matters, but people tend to operate with the knowledge that there is flexibility to these selections, since they can be modified or updated relatively easily. Because there is not a high cost to presenting new stimuli, putting less effort into initial stimuli selection and providing clarifications when needed can be an efficient means of engaging in the process of creating understanding.

However, when there are few opportunities for synchronous or reciprocal exchange, communicators are unlikely or unable to change stimuli once they have been selected. As a result, stimuli in minimally reciprocal and/or asynchronous situations tend to be more *static*. In these situations, communicators' choices in initial stimuli selection are more important, because they have limited opportunities to revise them later. In these situations, communicators often take more time and/or conscious effort to select stimuli. For example, professional writers often take considerable time to compose a written text: they draft and then revise their selection of stimuli many times, attempting to optimize its potential for activating desired meme states (given what they know about the text's audience). Once a text is written and published, there is little a writer can do if their audience does not find it "clear" (i.e. the audience experiences discrepancies between the meme states activated by the text and predictions by their situation models). Indeed, writers may never know if their audience ultimately arrives at the meme state(s) or situation model they originally intended.

In sum, we propose that the degrees of reciprocity and synchrony allowed by an interactional context affect how communicators approach stimuli selection in the process of creating understanding (i.e. as a rapid "guess and check" versus a more reflective approach). These factors can also affect how communicators address indications that their situation models may not be entrained successfully (i.e. ambiguities and potential misunderstandings). This is because reciprocity and synchrony shape communicators' ability to provide feedback and present new stimuli.

Generally, we propose that across interactive contexts, people engage in the same fundamental process when they create understanding (outlined in Chapter 5). However, in nonreciprocal—and to a lesser extent, asynchronous—contexts, people typically engage in all of the process internally, without each other's input. Given this constraint, it is perhaps not surprising that misunderstandings (i.e. situations in which communicators do not successfully entrain their situation models) seem to occur more frequently in nonreciprocal or asynchronous contexts.

Communication Medium

Another element of the communication context that can influence how people create understanding is the *communication medium*. In theory, research, and everyday discussions involving communication, variations on the term "medium" are used in variety of different ways and forms. "The media" can refer to the broadcasting industry or journalism, that is, a loose "set of media institutions" (Chaffee & Metzger, 2001, p. 366). Social media platforms such as Facebook, Twitter, and Instagram have been referred to as "media" in research (e.g. Bossetta, 2018; Javornik, 2016). In the arts community, a primary question asked is, "What medium do you work in?" When communication researchers compare different forms of communication, they sometimes claim that nonverbal communication is more "immediate" than verbal communication because the latter is more "cognitively mediated" (e.g. Andersen, 1999). Most researchers and scholars refer to communicative behavior that employs information or communication technologies as "mediated" communication. (This, in turn, implies that communication without such technologies, that is, face-to-face communication, is *unmediated*—a frequent claim that we contend is not accurate).

As these examples highlight, the term "media" is used to refer to a number of different, related concepts in communication scholarship. Generally, scholars appear to use the term intuitively; indeed, it is common to see studies use the term extensively without ever defining it (e.g. Park & Lee, 2019; Vonbun-Feldbauer & Matthes, 2018). To address the role of media—more specifically, a *communication medium*—in creating understanding, we wish to articulate a more narrowly focused definition of the term. We see a communication medium serving two primary functions. First, a communication medium allows people to distribute stimuli across time and space (i.e. from Point A to Point B, and from Time 1 to Time 2). Second, a communication medium allows communicators to present stimuli to one another (in order to activate meme states).

Accordingly, and for our purposes, we define a communication medium as any material or portion of the electromagnetic spectrum that can be systematically altered by a communicator with sufficient stability to (a) preserve stimuli or (b) cast stimuli accessible to human senses into the proximal environment of another communicator. This definition is consistent with the Latin origins of the word, which refer to something "in the middle" or between two (or more) things. As we define it, a medium is the physical instantiation "in the middle" between two or more communicators, through which they communicate.

In what follows, we focus primarily on the second function of a communication medium in our definition—allowing communicators to present stimuli to one another—because it is most pertinent to the process of creating understanding as we model it. We consider the particulars of stimuli distribution via different media (e.g. air, copper cable, fiber optic cable, microwave radiation, paper, magnetic tape, stone, plastic disks, etc.) as primarily being the province of engineers and information scientists. Although it is critically important to the process of communicating, an analysis of the distribution function of media (particularly in the 21st century) is beyond the scope of this book.

As we have defined it, a medium in and of itself does not necessarily have communicative value; that is, not all physical materials or portions of the electromagnetic spectrum that *can* be used for communication *are* used in this way. For instance, a blank white sheet of paper has the capacity to serve as a communication medium. However, in most situations, the paper's communicative value is only potential in its blank state. A medium is typically altered in some systematic fashion to play a role in the process of communicating. Thus, the moment someone makes a mark on that blank paper with pencil, the graphite marks and paper together function as a system and people have a medium with communicative value (i.e. a *communication* medium).

Functional communication media typically consist of a constant background and a variable foreground. For the purposes of simplicity, regardless of how many different physical materials or portions of the electromagnetic spectrum are jointly employed in this way, we will use the singular term "medium" to refer to the *integrated system* of constant and variable, used operationally to communicate. When people speak, air is their communication medium: they disrupt the relatively constant air pressure, creating compression waves with their voices that ultimately reach other people's ear drums. People can use a stick to make grooves and divots in a uniform sand or dirt surface to draw maps or write words. In skywriting, a plane leaves a systematic exhaust trail spelling out words against the constant background of the sky.

Systematically altering a medium in this manner is generally the means by which communicators create stimuli intended for other communicators.[1] From this follows an important point: *communication always requires a medium*. As discussed in Chapter 2, the only access people have to each other's minds is through their senses, so they must employ stimuli to activate, ascertain, and/or coordinate their mental representations (i.e. meme states, situation models). A communication medium enables users to create stimuli; thus, people need a medium to communicate, and by extension to create understanding. Viewed this way, no form of communication—including face-to-face interaction, should be thought of as "unmediated" communication.[2] Anyone who has taught a class or delivered a speech is likely aware one has to speak louder, and gesture larger, when speaking in an auditorium compared to a smaller room. This is, in part, because of the properties of air as a communication medium. If people in such situations want their audience to be able to perceive the stimuli they generate, those stimuli—for example, vocal and kinesic behavior—must overcome the dissipation of stimuli that naturally occurs across air as a medium.

Affordances

The form stimuli take and the way(s) in which those stimuli are accessible to communicators are both influenced by the affordances provided by a communication medium. We use the term *affordances* to refer to capacities or qualities of an object that enable different uses for that object (Gibson, 2015; Greeno, 1994; Jones, 2003). In what follows, we briefly discuss two affordances of media that relate to interfacing with social stimuli, and how these affordances can affect the process of creating understanding.

First, we can consider a medium's *available modalities*. Different communication media allow access to stimuli by different combinations of senses, or sensory modalities. We can compare and contrast different communication media in terms of which, and how many, modalities they make available. For example, hard copy books, magazines, letters, offer both visual and tactile stimuli (though the latter is used infrequently in most communication via these media). Air, which is the medium for a typical face-to-face conversation, offers the potential for auditory stimuli and, if people are sufficiently close, tactile and olfactory stimuli as well.

Available modalities can affect the process of creating understanding indirectly. Generally, the more modalities a medium affords, the more options communicators have for creating, presenting, and perceiving stimuli (Daft & Lengel, 1986). This allows for more complex communication events, and may help or hamper understanding (Dennis & Kinney, 1998). Multiple modalities can potentially aid the process of creating understanding by allowing for redundancy across modalities. Redundancy increases the likelihood that one's interlocutor will perceive stimuli that are presented, particularly if one mode is compromised (e.g. speaking in a loud room, where auditory stimuli might be hard to discern). If the stimuli presented across multiple modalities are redundant or complementary in what they activate, this can potentially help communicators activate the meme states they intend more readily (Fasoli et al., 2016). This, in turn, can facilitate the entrainment of situation models.

However, having multiple available modalities also creates the potential for ambiguity (e.g. Daft & Lengel, 1986; Fasoli et al., 2016). If stimuli presented across different modalities activate multiple contradictory or conflicting meme states, communicators are likely to experience confusion or uncertainty about what their interlocutor intends. This can inhibit the successful entrainment of communicators' situation models, and thus hinder the creation of understanding. Contradictions or conflicts should be less likely to occur if communicators have only a single modality. With that said, we do recognize that there can still be conflicts in multiple streams of stimuli even within a single modality. For example, spoken words and tone, both of which are auditory, can activate different meme states. In short, available modalities affect what stimuli communicators can use. In turn, how available stimuli are used (i.e. whether they reinforce activation of the same meme state or activate different, conflicting meme states) can affect the ease or difficulty with which people create understanding.

A second affordance we can consider is the *persistence* of stimuli in a given medium (e.g. Walther, 2017). If a medium can store stimuli, it allows those stimuli to persist over time. Spoken words are ephemeral; once they are spoken, they are gone (i.e. they do not persist). If people do not hear a word or a phrase in conversation, they cannot rewind and replay it. However, words in a book are available to revisit: if people miss a word or phrase, they can go back and re-read a sentence or paragraph quite easily. Unless the book (i.e. medium) itself gets damaged, people can return to exactly the same passage weeks, months, or years later.

Persistence of stimuli allows communicators to review and return to stimuli in their original form (or close) at later points in time (Walther, 2017). This enables review and/or reconsideration of those stimuli. If people's experiences of meme state activation are problematic (i.e. there are discrepancies between their situation model's prediction and the meme state initially activated), being able to revisit the stimuli could be helpful for resolving ambiguities. Communicators might have additional or different meme states active at a later point in time (as a result of exposure to different stimuli in the interim) that might help them determine which meme state their interlocutor intended, or allow for the activation of a different meme state than was activated initially. This has the potential to facilitate creating understanding. For example, re-reading a section of a textbook after attending a corresponding lecture, students may find they are better able to comprehend content they initially found confusing (i.e. they are better able to construct a situation model that corresponds to the situation model that the author had in mind when writing the book, or that the instructor had in mind when lecturing, than they were able to at a previous point in time).

Closely related, being able to revisit stimuli also allows people to reproduce or recreate experiences of meme state activation and/or a situation model they have experienced in the past. This can potentially facilitate creating understanding in a different situation later, or can help people consolidate or reinforce a situation model that corresponded to their fellow communicators' model at a previous point in time. For example, reviewing notes from class may help students reconstruct the experiences of meme state activation they previously had class. This, in turn, could help them (re)create a situation model of course content similar to their instructor's.

In sum, the affordances associated with different communication media can both facilitate and hinder creating understanding. The affordances we have discussed are just examples, we want to emphasize that this is not a comprehensive picture of possible factors related to communication media that could influence understanding. In this discussion, we have also focused on a relatively narrow conceptualization of the term "medium," addressing how communicators use media to interface with social stimuli. There may be other ways to conceptualize how people interface with social stimuli—particularly as communication technology continues to evolve and become more ubiquitous—and these different conceptualizations may highlight other factors that affect understanding. We see exploring these issues as important and interesting directions for future work on this topic.

Social and Cultural Norms

A third element of the communication context that can influence how people create understanding is social and cultural norms. All interactions take place in the context of a social situation that includes the social roles and statuses of participants; all interactions also take place within a broader cultural context (e.g. Dragojevic et al., 2016; Gallois et al., 2005). At each of these levels, there are norms for behavior that affect how people interact (Kim, 2005). Among other things, these norms can affect the nature and extent of stimuli that communicators present, including the extent to which communicators engage in interactive (as opposed to internal) disambiguation or error correction, as well as the meme states that specific stimuli activate for communicators. In short, social and cultural norms can be seen as a "filter" affecting stimuli selection, and a moderator of meme state activation.

Broadly, social and cultural norms provide guidelines on what communicators "should" say or do in social interaction. In some cases, these guidelines can follow from specific social identities or social roles that are salient in a given situation (e.g. Giles, 2012; Giles & Maas, 2016). For example, in a job interview, the interviewer typically asks questions and a job candidate responds until they are invited to ask their own questions. In some organizations, workers in subordinate roles are discouraged from questioning or challenging statements from their superiors. Similarly, in some cultures, younger adults are not supposed to question statements or assertions by their elders. In addition to following from salient social identities or social roles, social and cultural norms can also address more general tendencies or expectations for the nature of communication shared by members of a community (Kim, 2005). For example, different cultures have different norms for how socially acceptable it is to behave in a direct or indirect manner (e.g. Kim, 2012; Liu et al., 2011).

Social and cultural norms effectively impose bounds or constraints on the nature and extent of stimuli that communicators present. For example, in cultural contexts that favor indirect communication, communicators may not consider statements like, "I'm not going to do that" as possible or viable sets of stimuli they could present to evoke the meme state of a refusal. Such constraints on stimuli selection imposed by norms can occur at either a conscious level or a subconscious level. In some cases, communicators are aware of these constraints and consciously adapt their stimuli selection accordingly (e.g. "I really want to tell my boss that I disagree, but I know that is not how we do things at this company"). However, in other cases, it may not even occur to communicators that they could select a different set of stimuli that does not conform to social or cultural norms in context.

While the nature and extent of the constraints that norms introduce can vary across different social situations and cultures, we contend that all communicators experience some kind of constraints on stimuli selection by cultural and social norms. Because selection and presentation of stimuli is an integral part of the process of communicating, these constraints have implications for creating understanding.

First, adhering to social and cultural norms may lead people to select and present stimuli in ways that may not be optimized for creating understanding of content. One way this can manifest is by affecting the extent to which communicators engage in interactive (as opposed to internal) disambiguation or error correction. For example, if the local norm is that subordinates should not question their superiors, subordinates may be less likely to ask their superior for clarification when they are uncertain of what that superior has said or requested. Similarly, research on doctor-patient communication has found that patients often do not feel comfortable asking doctors for additional information or clarification when understanding has not successfully been created in a medical consultation. This is often attributed to the communication norms associated with the power and status differentials, as well as social identities that characterize doctor-patient interactions (Baker et al., 2017).

Even in situations without salient power or status imbalances, more general social norms typically limit the extent to which people seek clarification or ask meta-communicative questions. While people are generally willing to ask an interlocutor to repeat or rephrase what has been presented up to two or three times, more than that is (normatively) discouraged in most contexts. As a result, even if communicators have not successfully created understanding after a few attempts at interactive disambiguation, they often stop explicitly requesting (and providing) additional information of this sort, even if the interactive context objectively allows for it.

Second, social and cultural norms can also affect what specific stimuli activate for communicators. As described in Chapter 4, the associations that communicators have between stimuli and meme states are a product of experience. When people are from similar backgrounds (e.g. the same cultural or social group), they may be more likely to share sets of stimuli-meme state associations with one another that are a product of similar past experiences. Additionally, because most social behavior people experience within a social and cultural group is normative behavior, their associations between stimuli and meme states generally reflect the norms of their social and/or cultural group(s). For example, if both communicators in a conversation are members of cultures that favor indirect statements, the meme states activated by phrases like "maybe" or "I will take that under consideration" will reflect this cultural norm. The meme states activated by those phrases will also likely differ from what those statements activate for people from cultures that favor direct statements. Similarly, stimuli like tone of voice or use of artifacts may activate different meme states in cultural contexts that favor higher versus lower degrees of context dependence and/or directness in language use. In this way, social and cultural norms indirectly affect meme state activation.

Additionally, and closely related, people generally assume that other people will behave in normative ways in interaction. As such, social and cultural norms also inform communicators' expectations for each other's behavior. According to our framework, such expectations are reflected in communicators' situation models for an interaction. As described in the previous chapter, communicators' situation models can prime the activation of particular meme states; they also offer predictions for what will happen next in an interaction (and these predictions play a central in the process of meme state activation). Thus, social and cultural norms can also inform what meme states specific stimuli activate via their role in situation models.

Communicator Goals

Finally, a fourth element of the communication context that can influence how people create understanding is the goals of the people involved. In Chapter 4, we proposed that once people (implicitly) consent to communicate, they assume they are pursuing a shared goal of creating understanding. This shared assumption is important because it prompts people to use stimuli in ways that they believe will activate the meme states they desire or intend in their interlocutors' minds, and to treat the stimuli that their interlocutor presents as evidence of the meme states that person has in mind (Sperber & Wilson, 1995). In most cases, we contend, communicators are genuinely trying to create understanding, or entrain their situation models with their fellow interactants. Our discussions of understanding so far have primarily addressed, and focused on, such cases.

However, in a subset of situations, people may not have, or share, the goal of entraining most aspects of their situation models. In some cases, communicators may simply wish to prevent understanding—that is, they may want to disrupt or avert the process of entrainment. For example, parents sometimes wish to communicate with each other about topics like dessert or naps without their children understanding. In other cases, people may wish to deceive their interlocutor(s)—that is, they want to foster the construction of an alternative situation model to one they believe is true. For instance, a teenager may wish to make his parents think he was studying with friends the previous evening, when he was actually at a social event. In still other cases, people may want to influence or persuade someone else—that is, they want to strategically lead their partner to a particular situation model (see below).

In the domain of interpersonal communication research, multiple goal theories of communication (e.g. Wilson & Caughlin, 2018) highlight that communicators often have more than one (specific) goal that they are pursuing when they communicate with others. For example, people may want to seek an answer to a question, foster a positive relationship, and promote or protect a positive image of themselves simultaneously. Depending how these goals are prioritized, we propose that communicators will approach interactions in different ways, strategically selecting stimuli to activate particular meme states in line with their highest (or higher) priority goal(s). In some cases, interpersonal or relational goals may take precedence over the goal of creating understanding about specific content. For example, people might respond to a question (e.g. "Do you like my new dress?") minimally or ambiguously (e.g. "Green suits you well"), rather than explicitly, if they are prioritizing relational harmony, and are concerned that entraining situation models on dimensions that include their true opinions or beliefs pose a threat to that goal.

Similarly, in intergroup communication—that is, communication in circumstances where social identity is salient and influences how people communicate (e.g. Giles, 2012; Giles & Harwood, 2018; Giles & Maas, 2016)—communicators' prioritization of goals can affect how they engage in creating understanding. Communication accommodation theory (CAT) proposes that communication serves two functions: managing comprehension and managing social relationships, at both interpersonal and intergroup levels (Dragojevic et al., 2016). CAT also notes that these functions can be interrelated. Research on intergroup communication demonstrates that people's efforts to define group boundaries can affect the extent to which they sincerely seek to create understanding: one quite effective way to underscore outgroup status or exclude people from a group can be to prevent or disrupt understanding (Baker et al., 2017).

We argue that the basic processing of creating understanding that we propose holds across situations involving different communicator goals. Within this general process, however, the stimuli selected, the content of meme states activated, and the nature of adjustments made to situation models can and will be influenced by communicators' goals, and how they are prioritized. As discussed in Chapters 2 and 4, communicators' goals inform the nature and content of their situation models, both initially and throughout the interaction (e.g. Braver, 2012). If communicators prioritize creating understanding as a goal, they should be more willing and likely to invest cognitive resources in this process (e.g. Miller & Cohen, 2001; Petty & Cacioppo, 1986). This could manifest in investing more effort in selecting stimuli that they believe are relevant to their interlocutor. This could also involve engaging more effort in the process of meme state activation, particularly disambiguation and error correction when needed.

Following our model, if one communicator's goal is to prevent or derail the process of understanding, that person can present stimuli that do not fully correspond to the meme states and/or situation model that she has in mind. If a communicator's goal is simply to prevent understanding, she can present stimuli in communicatively uncooperative ways (see Chapter 4). In other words, she can present stimuli in ways she knows or expects to be unconventional or uninterpretable for her interlocutor (e.g. using terms or speaking a language that her interlocutor does not know; ignoring stimuli presented by an interlocutor and thus limiting the social stimuli she presents). These "uncooperative" stimuli will still activate meme states for her interlocutor. However, the content of the meme states activated, and the situation models fostered, are unlikely to be entrained with any specific content that the uncooperative communicator has in mind. In such situations, communicators may ultimately entrain on other dimensions of their situation models that capture the notion that one communicator does not want to create understanding. Indeed, if one communicator's efforts to prevent understanding (of specific content) are successful, communicators may create understanding about the fact that there will be no further efforts to create understanding.

When communicators prioritize other (e.g. social) goals than understanding, we contend that communicators will still seek to entrain their situation models (i.e. create understanding) to some degree. However, the extent and nature of entrainment will be moderated by communicators' goals. We have argued that in creating understanding, communicators entrain their situation models (only) to the extent required for their present purposes (Chapter 2). Communicators' goals contribute to defining and circumscribing these "present purposes". When communicators have goals other than content understanding, their situation models also include content relating to these alternative goals (e.g. expressing that one cares about another person; being seen in a positive light). In situations where those alternative goals are prioritized, entraining these aspects or dimensions of communicators' situation models may be emphasized over other aspects of the situation model, such as factual content. This, in turn, will be reflected in the stimuli communicators select, present, observe, and process.

In line with this, persuasion and/or social influence can be seen as a specific case of creating understanding as a more general process. A communicator who wishes to influence or persuade essentially seeks to cultivate a specific situation model in their interlocutor's mind. (Typically, this intended situation model is different than the model their interlocutor had before the persuasive interaction). In such an interaction, a communicator will focus on entraining the dimensions of the situation model that relate specifically to his persuasive goals. In some cases, people may want their persuasive intent to remain covert; if this is the case, they would actively avoid entraining this (pragmatic) dimension of their situation model with their interlocutors'. If people are not concerned with persuasive intent being overt, then this may also be a dimension on which seek to entrain their situation models (e.g. making explicit that they are trying to convince someone to support a candidate).

Finally, in the case of deception, a communicator may have a specific, alternative (to truth) situation model that they wish their interlocutor(s) to construct or experience. In this situation, the deceptive communicator has a two-part situation model in mind, consisting of both (a) what she knows to be true and (b) the alternative (fictive) account she wishes her interlocutor to believe. In interaction, the deceptive communicator seeks to entrain only part (b) of her situation model, so the stimuli she presents should correspond, and seek to activate, specific meme states that correspond (only) to this part of her overall situation model. Deceptive communicators also actively avoid entraining on the dimension(s) of their situation model addressing deceptive intent. Thus, from the perspective of our framework, "successful" deception consists of deliberately managed entrainment of specific aspects of situation models between communicators.

Summary

In this chapter, we have discussed how some contextual features—specifically, the interactive context, the medium of communication, social and cultural norms, and communicators' goals—can affect how people enact and experience the process of creating understanding. From this, we highlight two points. First, the framework we provide offers a process model that is fundamentally stable across contexts. That is, the core processes we describe occur regardless of variance in contextual factors. However, and second, sub-processes in the model we have outlined (e.g. stimuli selection, disambiguation and error correction), as well as situation-specific instantiations and content of its components (e.g. situation models, meme states activated) can be affected by the context of an interaction, in various forms and at multiple levels.

In the preceding pages, we have focused on just a few contextual factors that can affect creating understanding. There are certainly many other factors that also can and do influence how people enact and experience the processes we have outlined in this book: communicators' dispositions (i.e. personalities), individual interests or preferences, and affective states are just a few of many possible examples. While we cannot comprehensively address all variables that could possibly affect creating understanding, we hope the examples we have provided here highlight ways in which specific components of the model we have proposed may be influenced and moderated by contextual factors.

Notes

1. We note that people can sometimes use a *lack* of alteration to a medium (where one would be anticipated) to present stimuli. For instance, a student might turn in a blank assignment as a

form of protest, or an artist might hang a blank canvas in a gallery as an artistic statement. In these cases, we propose that actors are essentially creating stimuli by manipulating the *expectation* of a variable foreground on a constant background, in light of an interlocutor's active situation model. The stimuli themselves are still rendered via the medium (e.g. the sheet of paper or the canvas) as a physical material. This manipulation of expectations to produce social stimuli is possible because (a) people are capable of predictive inference-making—that is, predicting that things should happen a particular way (Chapter 3: Premise 3); and (b) people are capable of mentalizing (Chapter 3: Premise 1)—that is, recognizing that other people have expectations, and thus that acting contrary to those expectations will have particular effects.

2. In thinking about this process, it is important to remember that what people subjectively experience as "direct" interaction with the world is always and only experienced through their senses. People's senses sample from the world external to them and that sampling—through touch, vision, hearing, smell, and taste—only corresponds to what their senses are able to process. Vast portions of the world external to human bodies (e.g. x-rays, infrared light, ultrasonic frequencies) are unavailable to people's conscious experiences due to the limitations of the human senses. For example, at any moment, most people today are literally immersed in communicative media—microwaves, radio waves, infrared signals—carrying gigabytes of messages that are completely invisible to them.

We propose that one way to think about this issue is to consider the senses that people come into the world with as *first-order* sensory technology. With the help of *second-order* sensory technology, it is possible to restore damaged first-order sensory technology to a standard, or "normative", state: glasses, contact lenses, and hearing aids are all examples of this. Finally, people have also developed what we term *third-order* sensory technology, or technologies that augment or amplify human senses beyond their normal capabilities. Examples of these include microscopes, binoculars, and telescopes; or glasses/goggles that sample from electromagnetic spectra not visible to unaided eyes, allowing people to see in the dark or see infrared radiation. Optical aids that allow people to see digital information overlaid on their field of vision are also examples of this. For our purposes, we consider anything accessing and/or accessible to our senses—regardless of the technology used to have this experience—a communication medium functioning as a sensory interface.

References

Andersen, P. A. (1999). *Nonverbal communication: Forms and functions*. Mayfield Publishing.

Baker, S., Watson, B. M., & Gallois, C. (2017). Exploring intercultural communication problems in health care with a communication accommodation competence approach. In L. Chen (Ed.), *Intercultural Communication*, Volume 9 of *Handbooks of communication science* (pp. 481-499). Mouton de Gruyter. https://doi.org/10.1515/9781501500060-022

Bossetta, M. (2018). The digital architectures of social media: Comparing political campaigning on Facebook, Twitter, Instagram, and Snapchat in the 2016 U.S. election. *Journalism & Mass Communication Quarterly, 95*(2), 471-496. https://doi.org/10.1177/1077699018763307

Braver, T. S. (2012). The variable nature of cognitive control: A dual mechanisms framework. *Trends in Cognitive Sciences, 16*(2), 106–113. https://doi.org/10.1016/j.tics.2011.12.010

Burgoon, J. K., Dunbar, N. E., & Giles, H. (2017). Interaction coordination and adaptation. In J. K. Burgcon, N. Magnenat-Thalmann, M. Pantic, & A. Vinciarelli (Eds.), *Social signal processing* (pp. 78–96). Cambridge University Press. https://doi.org/10.1017/9781316676202.008

Chaffee, S. H., & Metzger, M. J. (2001). The end of mass communication. *Mass Communication & Society, 4*(4), 365–379. https://doi.org/10.1207/S15327825MCS0404_3

Clark, H. H. (1996). *Using language.* Cambridge University Press. https://doi.org/10.1017/CBO9780511620539

Clark, H. H., & Brennan, S. E. (1991). Grounding in communication. In L. B. Resnick, J. M. Levine, & S. D. Teasley (Eds.), *Perspectives on socially shared cognition,* (pp. 127–149). American Psychological Association. https://doi.org/10.1037/10096-006

Clark, H. H., & Krych, M. A. (2004). Speaking while monitoring addressees for understanding. *Journal of Memory and Language, 50*(1), 62–81. https://doi.org/10.1016/j.jml.2003.08.004

Daft, R. L., & Lengel, R. H. (1986). Organizational information requirements, media richness, and structural design. *Management Science, 32*(5), 554–571. https://doi.org/10.1287/mnsc.32.5.554

Dennis, A. R., & Kinney, S. T. (1998). Testing media richness theory in new media: The effects of cues, feedback, and task equivocality. *Information Systems Research, 9*(3), 256–274. https://doi.org/10.1287/isre.9.3.256

Dennis, A. R., Fuller, R. M., & Valacich, J. S. (2008). Media, tasks, and communication processes: A theory of media synchronicity. *MIS Quarterly, 32*(3), 575–600. https://doi.org/10.2307/25148857

Dragojevic, M., Gasiorek, J., & Giles, H. (2016). Accommodative strategies as core of CAT. In H. Giles (Ed.), *Communication accommodation theory: Negotiating personal and social identities across contexts* (pp. 36–59). Cambridge University Press. https://doi.org/10.1017/CBO9781316226537.003

Fasoli, F., Maass, A., & Sulpizio, S. (2016). Communication of the "invisible": Disclosing and inferring sexual orientation through visual and vocal cues. In H. Giles & A. Maass (Eds.), *Advances in intergroup communication* (pp. 193–208). Peter Lang.

Gallois, C., Ogay, T., & Giles, H. (2005). Communication accommodation theory: A look back and a look ahead. In W. B. Gudykunst (Ed.), *Theorizing about intercultural communication* (pp. 121–148). SAGE.

Garrod, S., Fay, N., Lee, J., Oberlander, J., & MacLeod, T. (2007). Foundations of representation: Where might graphical symbol systems come from? *Cognitive Science, 31,* 961–987. https://doi.org/10.1080/03640210701703659

Gibson, J. J. (2015). *The ecological approach to visual perception: Classic edition.* Psychology Press.

Giles, H. (Ed.). (2012). *The handbook of intergroup communication*. Routledge. https://doi.org/10.4324/9780203148624

Giles, H., & Harwood, J. (Eds.). (2018). *Oxford encyclopedia of intergroup communication* (Volumes 1 and 2). Oxford University Press. https://doi.org/10.1093/acref/9780190454524.001.0001

Giles, H. & Maass, A. (Eds.) (2016). *Advances in intergroup communication*. Peter Lang. https://doi.org/10.3726/b10467

Greeno, J. G. (1994). Gibson's affordances. *Psychological Review, 101*(2), 336–342. https://doi.org/10.1037/0033-295X.101.2.336

Haeckel, S. H. (1998). About the nature and future of interactive marketing. *Journal of Interactive Marketing, 12*(1), 63–71. https://doi.org/10.1002/(SICI)1520-6653(199824)12:1%3C63::AID-DIR8%3E3.0.CO;2-C

Javornik, A. (2016). Augmented reality: Research agenda for studying the impact of its media characteristics on consumer behavior. *Journal of Retailing and Consumer Services, 30*, 252–261. http://dx.doi.org/10.1016/j.jretconser.2016.02.004.

Jones, K. S. (2003). What is an affordance? *Ecological Psychology, 15*(2), 107–114. https://doi.org/10.1207/S15326969ECO1502_1

Kim, M. S. (2002). *Non-Western perspectives on human communication*. SAGE.

Kim, Y. Y. (2005). Inquiry in intercultural and development communication. *Journal of Communication, 55*(3), 554–577. https://doi.org/10.1111/j.1460-2466.2005.tb02685.x

Liu, S., Volčič, Z., & Gallois, C. (2011). *Introducing intercultural communication: Global cultures and contexts*. SAGE.

Miller, E. K., & Cohen, J. D. (2001). An integrative theory of prefrontal cortex function. *Annual Review of Neuroscience, 24*, 167–202. https://doi.org/10.1146/annurev.neuro.24.1.167

Park, Y. W., & Lee, A. R. (2019). The moderating role of communication contexts: How do media synchronicity and behavioral characteristics of mobile messenger applications affect social intimacy and fatigue? *Computers in Human Behavior, 97*, 179–192. https://doi.org/10.1016/j.chb.2019.03.020

Petty, R. E., & Cacioppo, J. T. (1986). The elaboration likelihood model of persuasion. In L. Berkowitz (Ed.), *Advances in experimental social psychology* (*Vol. 19*, pp. 213–205). Academic Press. https://doi.org/10.1016/S0065-2601(08)60214-2

Sperber, D., & Wilson, D. (1995). *Relevance: Communication and cognition (2nd Ed.)*. Blackwell.

Stromer-Galley, J. (2004). Interactivity-as-product and interactivity-as-process. *The Information Society, 20*(5), 391–394. https://doi.org/10.1080/01972240490508081

Vonbun-Feldbauer, R., & Matthes, J. (2018). Do channels matter? *Journalism Studies, 19*, 2359–2378. https://doi.org/10.1080/1461670X.2017.1349547

Walther, J. B. (2017). The merger of mass and interpersonal communication via new media: Integrating metaconstructs. *Human Communication Research, 43*(4), 559–572. https://doi.org/10.1111/hcre.12122

Wilson, S. R., & Caughlin, J. P. (2018). Multiple goals theories: Motivations for family interactions and relationships. In D. C. Braithwaite, E. A. Suter, & K. Floyd (Eds.), *Engaging theories in family communication: Multiple perspectives* (2nd ed., pp. 199–209). Routledge. https://doi.org/10.4324/9781315204321-18

CHAPTER SEVEN

Codification

This chapter focuses on the role of codified communication systems (historically, "codes") in creating understanding. We briefly discuss the limitations of current approaches to the topic in the discipline of communication, and then offer an alternative perspective. Specifically, we propose that it is more useful to focus on codification as a descriptive continuum and as a process, rather than "codes" as discrete categories and products. We outline key properties of codification, offer a set of examples illustrating how these properties manifest in different communication systems, and then address correlates of codification relevant to creating understanding. We then discuss how codified communicative systems develop, arguing that they emerge as a result of the three premises we have outlined: human beings' fundamental social orientation, predisposition toward efficiency, and engagement in predictive inference-making. Finally, we address the role of codified communication systems in creating understanding.

The concept of a "codes" is regularly invoked in contemporary communication research and teaching: language is often referred to as "code", as are different domains of nonverbal behavior (e.g. "kinesic code", "proxemic code", etc.). In Chapter 5, we proposed a process model for how people create understanding in social interaction that included no references to codes. Thus, it is evidently possible to theorize about communication processes without codes. However, it is clear from everyday experience that people frequently do use sets of conventions that have code-like properties (e.g. language) to communicate, and to create understanding. In this chapter, we address such communication systems, discussing their nature and emergence, as well as the role they play in creating understanding. In this, we propose that a focus on *codification* in *communication systems*, rather than *codes*, is more theoretically accurate and productive; we also offer a novel perspective on these systems.

"Codes" in Communication Research

Classically, a code is a system in which one set of elements (e.g. words, numbers, symbols; stimuli) stands for, or refers to, another set (e.g. other words, numbers, or symbols; meme states). In an archetypal or prototypical code, there is one-to-one correspondence between these elements, such that a given stimulus corresponds to one and only one meme state. This description is consistent with codes such as Morse code, in which specific dots and dashes are rigidly associated with alphanumeric symbols. However, it is clearly inconsistent with the polysemy we see in human languages and nonverbal behavior; as such, much of what communication scholars have historically called "codes" does not fit a strict definition of the term. Nevertheless, people's observable communicative behavior often does involve using stimuli in relatively standardized and systematic ways, and drawing on associations between stimuli and the meme states. This occurs across different domains or categories of communicative behavior, from language to bodily movements to the use of artifacts.

How did communication researchers come to refer to these sets of conventions as "codes"? One likely source of this use of "code" (and related terms like "encoding" and "decoding") in contemporary communication scholarship is Shannon and Weaver's (1949) model of digital communication. As discussed in Chapter 1, although this model was intended to address signal processing and transmission, communication scholars adopted (and adapted) it to describe the process of human communication. Drawing parallels to the process of signal transmission, scholars saw systems of human behavior used in communication (such as language) function in a similar manner to digital code, and the terminology followed accordingly. Widespread use of variations on the code model by communication scholars perpetuated and helped cement the idea that people used "codes" to communicate.

Another, related factor that may have contributed to communication scholars' emphasis on "codes" is the historical dominance of language in the study of communication. Dating back to at least the ancient Greeks (who wrote treatises on oratory and how rhetoric could move and motivate people), scholars interested in communication have focused primarily on how people use language. As the field (and discipline) of communication coalesced and emerged as a distinct academic area in the middle of the 20th century, some researchers began to investigate other aspects of face-to-face communication (e.g. Birdwhistell, 1971; Hall, 1966). This new area ultimately came to be labeled "nonverbal communication", and has become an established sub-field of communication research. However, because of language's dominant status, the manner in which researchers labeled, conceptualized and studied verbal communication—including the term "code"—was carried over to nonverbal communication. By the early 1970s, references to nonverbal "codes" could be commonly found throughout the scholarly literature on nonverbal communication (e.g. Burgoon & Saine, 1978; Ramsey, 1976; Wiener et al., 1972).

We suggest that this division of communication processes into "verbal" and "nonverbal" has had unintended consequences for the study of communication, and by extension, understanding. Because this set of two labels implicitly suggests a whole, it has inadvertently closed scholars' eyes to other systems of human communication[1] that are not classically verbal or nonverbal in nature—for instance, mathematical or musical notation, or the use of aesthetic conventions. The label of "*non*verbal" communication also implicitly accepts and perpetuates the privileged status of verbal communication (i.e. language).

Perhaps more importantly, we contend that this disciplinary focus on "codes" has shaped and ultimately constrained the way that scholars think about communication systems. First, focusing on "codes" has implicitly reinforced a code model view of communication, and by extension understanding, which is problematic (see Chapter 1). Second, the use of "code" to describe a wide range of different communication systems has resulted in ambiguity about what constitutes a "code", and how codes are conceptualized in communication research. Third, and finally, a focus on "codes" as discrete categories has (inadvertently) led communication researchers to focus on examining circumscribed sets of behavior (i.e. extant "codes" such as kinesics or proxemics), rather than theorizing about codified systems in more general terms, and studying how they emerge and develop. In the following sections, we aim to address these issues, offering a novel perspective that contextualizes systems of communicative behavior in a larger picture of how people communicate and create understanding.

Codification

As stated at the outset of this chapter, codes are classically defined as systems in which one set of elements (for our purposes, stimuli) is mapped to another set of elements (for our purposes, meme states), typically in a one-to-one fashion. Given that nearly all of "codes" that are employed in human communication do not actually conform to a strict definition of the term, we propose that communication scholars ought to change both their conceptual approach to this topic and their corresponding terminology. Specifically, we propose it is more productive to focus on *codification* as a descriptive continuum (i.e. the extent to which a set of communication conventions exhibits code-like qualities) and as a process (i.e. how sets of conventions exhibiting qualities of codes emerge and develop), than it is to focus on *codes* as discrete categories and products.

Because there is currently ambiguity about what constitutes or defines communication systems scholars have traditionally labeled "codes", it is also important to provide a clear conceptualization of codification, and what it entails. In what follows, we define the key properties of codification, offer a set of examples illustrating how these properties manifest in different communication systems, and then address correlates of codification relevant to communication and creating understanding. In this, we specifically address codification as it relates to human communication, and use the term "codification" as shorthand for "codification that occurs in the context and process of human communication."

Properties of Codification

Codified systems that have developed for human communication have a set of shared qualities or properties, which different systems (i.e. "codes") exhibit to varying degrees. In what follows, we briefly outline and discuss these qualities as *properties of codification*.

One property of codification is *reliable associations*. As the definition of a code indicates, codification entails stable connections between sets of elements in a system. In the case of communication, these are typically associations between a *feature configuration* (i.e. abstracted, essential formal and structural features of stimuli; see below) and a meme state. These reliable associations between feature configurations and meme states are the basic units of codified systems. With that said, these associations vary in their consistency. In some cases, associations between feature configurations and meme states in a system are very consistent (e.g. the association between a series of dots, dashes, and the letter or number they call to mind in Morse code). In other cases, they are less consistent (e.g. the association between a particular tone of voice and the notion of irony or sarcasm in vocalics). This variation in strength is a partial function of the frequency with which that specific association has been used, and therefore reinforced, in communicators' previous experience with that codified communication system.

As a result of the associations between feature configurations and meme states, a given feature configuration in a codified system consistently evokes similar meme states across different situations. The potential of a given feature configuration to activate a corresponding meme state can be seen as probabilistic, following from the consistency of their association. In highly codified systems, the probability of a feature configuration activating its associated meme state is high; this reflects strong, highly reliable links between feature configurations and meme states. In systems that are not as highly codified, the probability of a feature configuration activating its associated meme state is lower; this reflects weaker, less reliable links between feature configurations and meme states. Thus, in a (highly) codified system, the associations between feature configurations and meme states allow people to reliably activate specific meme states through the use of feature configurations. For example, for speakers of the English language, the word "dog" reliably activates the same meme state (i.e. a canine, typically domesticated) across people and across contexts.

Another property of codification is *formal and structural abstraction*. In a codified system, the essential formal and structural features of stimuli that activate a given meme state are distilled; this distillation occurs as a codified system develops. As we define it, a feature configuration consists of the combination of (a) the form (i.e. morphology) of essential features of a set of stimuli associated with a given meme and (b) the structural relationships between those essential features. Once an abstracted feature configuration is established, the stimuli that communicators use to activate a given meme are not necessarily tied to a specific instance or physical manifestation of those stimuli. As long as enough of the essential elements of the feature configuration are retained and recognized, people treat different manifestations or instantiations of a given feature configuration (i.e. different sets of physical stimuli) as equivalent or interchangeable. Generally, people do not need every single formal or structural feature that defines a feature configuration to be present for that feature configuration to function in a codified system. Rather, people just need the features available in a given set of stimuli to be sufficient to reach a threshold for recognition (and therefore meme activation) in context.

For example, the word "dog", which is part of the codified system of the written English language, can be written in pen, pencil, or crayon on different types of paper; it can also manifest in pixels on a wide variety of different screens (e.g.

monitor, laptop, tablet, smartphone). These manifestations can vary in size; the word could be less than a square centimeter on paper or a small screen, or a square foot or more, if it is projected on a screen in a large lecture hall. However, people recognize and treat all these manifestations as being the "same" as long as they retain a set of essential formal and structural features. In the case of "dog", these essential features are the letters "d", "o", and "g", in that order, placed relatively close together.

We propose that these interrelated properties—reliable associations, consistent evocation according to associations, and formal abstraction—define codification in human communication. However, as alluded to above, different codified communication systems can and do exhibit these properties to different degrees. Because of this, we argue that it is best to consider and classify systems of conventions used in human communication along a *continuum of codification*. When a communication system exhibits these interrelated properties in a robust manner, the system can be considered *highly codified*; when it exhibits them less robustly, it can be considered *less* (or *minimally*) *codified*.

However, we argue that all of these properties must be present to at least some degree for communicators' use of stimuli to be considered codified. If these properties are not all present, people's use of stimuli to activate meme states is idiosyncratic—that is, people are using stimuli to evoke meme states in ways that are limited or peculiar to a single or specific situation. Idiosyncratic use of stimuli to evoke meme states can be an effective way to create understanding, but it is typically resource-intensive. As we discuss in greater detail below, this makes idiosyncratic use of stimuli unlikely as a sustained or long-term means of creating understanding. Instead, there is a tendency towards codification in human interaction.

The properties we have just outlined are essential to codification, but they are not the only characteristics that codified communication systems exhibit. In some, but not all, cases, codification can also involve *combinatorial feature configurations*—that is, it can be possible to create larger feature configuration units from a set of smaller units (Galantucci et al., 2010; Galantucci & Garrod, 2011). In many cases, combinatorial codified systems also exhibit *compositionality*—that is, both (a) the content of a combination of feature configuration units, and (b) the way these units are assembled contribute to the evocation of particular meme states (Smith et al., 2003). More specifically, in compositional systems, there generally are conventions for how smaller units can (and cannot) be assembled, and the way that units are assembled or arranged also has corresponding meme content. Grammar conventions in language, conventions for ordering symbols in mathematical notation, and the positioning of different symbols in modern musical notation are all examples of assembly conventions in communication systems.

Generally, in compositional systems, the meme state evoked by a larger unit that has been assembled according to the system's conventions is distinct from what each individual sub-unit would evoke. In other words, the higher order unit offers more than the sum of its parts. This allows the larger units that combined stimuli comprise to evoke specific, more complex meme states than each component of the stimuli might on its own. For example, "Sally walked the dog" evokes a different, and more complex, meme state than "Sally" "the dog", and "walked" do as independent units. Combinatorial use of stimuli and compositionality— and their corresponding conventions for combining stimuli—are not essential properties of codification. However, they do characterize some communication systems (including language), and generally increase those systems' flexibility and communicative power.

Examples of Codified Communication Systems

Before proceeding further, we want to offer some illustrations of communication systems with different degrees of codification (as well as compositionality) as illustrations of the properties we have outlined. We propose that when a set of communicative practices develop that enable people to reliably activate specific meme states via particular feature configurations, it is an instance of a communication system that falls somewhere on the continuum of codification.

Mathematical notation and modern musical notation are examples of highly codified communication systems. Mathematical notation refers to how math is written, including numbers, symbols for mathematical operations, and notation used in proofs (e.g. "QED"). Modern musical notation refers to standardized conventions for how music is written, including information about the order and length of notes, time signature, key, and more. In these systems, there are highly reliable associations between feature configurations and memes, such that feature configurations consistently evoke highly similar meme states across different people and in different situations. For example, in modern musical notation, a whole note (i.e. a given visual feature configuration) always corresponds to playing a note for a full beat in the time signature (i.e. the same specific meme state and corresponding behavior).

As a result of this high degree of codification, mathematicians and musicians across the world experience highly similar meme states when they are given the same feature configurations. As discussed further below, highly codified systems such as these leave little to no room for implicature or inference-making, and an important part of their functional value is the high degree of consistency with which they activate meme states across communicators and contexts. Both mathematical and musical notation systems are also combinatorial and compositional; that is, they have well-defined conventions for how to combine feature configurations into larger units.

Kinesics and vocalics are examples of moderately codified systems. Kinesics refers to how people use their bodies as visual stimuli to activate meme states in others. (It is worth noting that this system does not require an actual physical body as a medium; it can include depictions of bodies, as in picture books or comics). Vocalics refers how people use the qualities of their voices[2] as auditory stimuli to activate meme states. This can include pitch, speech rate, intonation, vocal emphasis, pronunciation, volume, and degree of articulation (as just some examples). In communication systems like kinesics and vocalics, there are some reliable associations between feature configurations and specific meme states, but some associations are looser and/or less consistent.

As a result, in these systems, similar use of a given feature configuration will often, but not always, evoke similar meme states across different situations. For example, there are particular vocal intonation patterns that are frequently used to indicate sarcasm. However, these do not activate the meme state of "sarcasm" as reliably as a whole note in musical notation activates "play this note for a full beat in the time signature." Vocalics and kinesics are also less combinatorial and compositional: while different stimuli in the systems can be combined together, there are not necessarily well-defined conventions for doing so, and the way in which stimuli are combined does not necessarily or reliably contribute to meme state activation. As such, in these systems, the combination of different units of stimuli does not always activate something different or distinct from their sum.

Use of artifacts and aesthetics are examples of communication systems with relatively low levels of codification. Use of artifacts refers to how people systematically use physical objects to activate meme states for others. How people dress, what glasses or accessories they use, and how people manipulate and decorate their immediate environment (e.g. their office or workspace) can all be part of this communication system. Aesthetics refers to the ways in which various arts—for example, painting, sculpting, acting, dancing, music composition, music performance—systematically employ particular conventions in stimuli use to evoke particular meme states in others. (For a discussion of cognitive processing of art, and how it may be fundamentally similar to that of other forms of communication, see McCallum et al., 2020). For example, in the visual arts, artists strategically use warm colors to evoke different affective reactions than cool colors. In communication systems like aesthetics and use of artifacts, there are some established associations between feature configurations and specific meme states, but many are not highly reliable or consistent.

As a result of this low degree of codification, use of the same feature configurations does not always activate the same meme states across contexts. For example, use of cool colors in some situations can evoke sadness; in others, it might evoke serenity or calm. Additionally, there are few, if any, established conventions in such systems for how to combine stimuli into larger units, and the way stimuli are combined generally does not reliably contribute to meme state activation.

Finally, language as a communication system can also be placed along this continuum of codification.[3] (Language could be further reduced to *written (visual)* and *spoken (auditory)* communication systems). We consider language to have a moderately high degree of codification (i.e. greater than vocalics, but less than modern mathematical or musical notation). Language exhibits fairly reliable associations between feature configurations (typically, words) and specific meme states, such that words consistently evoke quite similar meme states in different situations. However, there is considerable polysemy in language: the same visual stimuli (e.g. written word "wind") can evoke different meme states in different contexts (e.g. the natural phenomenon of air moving, or the action of zig-zagging). Similarly, in spoken language, the same auditory stimuli (e.g. the combination of phonemes that creates "to", "too", and "two") can evoke different meme states in different contexts. This polysemy occurs on multiple levels. For instance, it is possible to construct larger units, like sentences, that follow grammatical conventions but can evoke multiple possible meme states (e.g. "I'm glad I'm here and so is Sally"). As a result of this polysemy, people given the same feature configurations as input can and often do have different meme states activated in different situations. It is also notable that language is also highly combinatorial and compositional. All human languages have well-developed systems of conventions for combining stimuli into larger units, although the content of the conventions differs between languages (Galantucci & Garrod, 2011; Pereltsvaig, 2012; Smith et al., 2003).

Correlates of Codification

Having established that different communication systems are codified to different degrees, we now turn to some of the consequences of codification. We address these as *correlates of codification*: that is, interrelated properties of communicative experiences that vary as the degree of codification varies.

Generally, as codification increases, so does the *consistency of people's response* to manifestations of feature configurations. This follows directly from the reliability of associations between feature configurations and meme states in codification. In highly codified systems, these associations are highly fixed, and therefore reliable, so the same feature configurations consistently evoke the same meme states across situations. Closely related, meme states that are "encoded" using that communication system are usually "decoded" in a highly similar fashion across multiple, different communicators. For example, nearly any reader of a written mathematical equation will experience the same meme states being activated, as long as they have sufficient knowledge of mathematical notation as a codified communication system and corresponding conceptual knowledge of mathematics. The meme states this written equation activates (i.e. the "decoding" of the equation) should also correspond with the meme states the equation's author had when writing (i.e. "encoding") it.

A second, related correlate is *context dependence*. Generally, as codification decreases, the contribution of contextual stimuli to meme state activation (and by extension, creating understanding) increases. As described in Chapter 4, contextual stimuli contribute to meme state activation by making some meme states more accessible than others (i.e. lowering the amount of processing effort required for their activation). This is more consequential in situations where a feature configuration could potentially evoke multiple, different meme states. Such situations, in turn, occur more frequently when people use communication systems with lower degrees of codification. For example, contextual stimuli contribute heavily to what meme states are activated by a gesture such as pointing (which could activate "look more closely at this", "watch out for this", or "I am referring to this particular object", among many possibilities). In contrast, contextual stimuli contribute minimally to what meme states are activated by a mathematical equation.

A third, closely related correlate is the *flexibility of stimuli use*. Generally, as codification decreases, communicators have greater potential flexibility in what they can use a given set of stimuli to evoke (via feature configurations) (Piantadosi et al., 2012). In highly codified systems, a given feature configuration evokes a very narrow set of meme states; in archetypal "codes", there is a one-to-one correspondence between feature configurations and meme states. However, in systems that are less codified, a given feature configuration (instantiated in a set of stimuli) can be used to evoke a wider variety of different meme states. (In this, contextual stimuli can play an important role in determining what meme state is activated, as just described). For example, when writing out mathematical equations, a plus sign (as a feature configuration in a highly codified system) can only be used to evoke the idea of adding two quantities together; there is virtually no flexibility. In contrast, pointing one's finger (as a feature configuration in a moderately codified system) can evoke a number of different possible meme states (e.g. "look more closely at this", "watch out for this", or "I am referring to this particular object", etc.). In short, in systems with lower degrees of codification, stimuli are more context dependent and can thus be used in more versatile ways.

Finally, and again related, the extent to which communicators engage in *inference-making* or *implicature* varies with codification. Generally, as codification increases, the degree of inference-making or implicature involved in using a given communication system decreases. Thus, in using highly codified systems, there is typically minimal inference-making in the meme activation process that follows from attending to feature configurations, as well as little to no implicature present in communicators' presentation of stimuli. In contrast, in systems that are less codified, feature configurations are not associated with meme states as reliably, stimuli can be used more flexibly, and communicators rely more heavily on context in the process of communicating. As such, people tend to engage in a higher degree of inference-making in meme state activation, and implicature in stimuli presentation.

Together, these four correlates offer some insight into the relative success and failure of computer systems to model various aspects of human communication. Computers easily handle highly codified systems, because responses to feature configurations are highly reliable, there is little to no dependence on context, and there is little flexibility or versatility in stimuli use. All of these characteristics allow a computer to be programmed to respond reliably to feature configurations in specific ways that are consistent with the codified system. Given these observations, it is not surprising that two functions that early computers were programmed to do were various mathematical activities and playing music. However, computers have had more difficulty reliably addressing behaviors like facial expressions or tone of voice, which are feature configurations from less codified communication systems. Although machine learning algorithms have enabled considerable strides in this area (e.g. Vinciarelli et al., 2017) it will likely be awhile before current commercial AI systems can show average adult human skills at responding appropriately to kinesic or vocalic communicative behavior.

Emergence and Development of Codification

We now turn our attention to how codified communication systems develop. Put another way, we ask: how does codification, as a process, occur? We propose that when people interact with the goal of creating understanding, codification follows from the three premises addressing human behavior and cognition outlined in Chapter 3: people's fundamental social orientation, their predisposition toward efficiency, and their use of predictive inference-making.

Before proceeding, we wish to emphasize that, in seeking to describe and explain how codification occurs, we focus on the present—that is, how codification arises in human communication in contemporary times. It is not intended as a theoretical account of how codified systems (in particular, language) emerged on an evolutionary timescale (e.g. Reboul, 2015; Scott-Phillips, 2015; Tomasello, 2008). The origins of human language is a fascinating and active area of scholarship (some of which we draw on in this discussion), but addressing this larger question is not our goal, and is beyond the scope of this book.

There is a robust body of evidence that people develop codified systems for communication when they are faced with situations in which they do not have pre-established conventions or communication systems available to them, but want to communicate something (e.g. Theisen et al., 2010). In some cases, this happens on a large scale; for example, deaf children that are not taught a formalized signing system develop their own signing systems (e.g. Goldin-Meadow & Feldman, 1977; Goldin-Meadow, & Mylander, 1998). In other cases, this occurs on a smaller scale, within and across everyday interactions (and often, grounded in existing communication systems). Close friends, couples, and families often develop sets of shared communicative conventions (e.g. labels for objects or people) unique to their dyad or small group. Experimental research addressing the emergence of communication systems also offers evidence that codified systems develop when people are placed in situations where they need to communicate, but do not have access to existing systems (for a review, see Galantucci & Garrod, 2011).

We propose that people's capacity for (recursive) mentalizing—which is a manifestation of their fundamental social orientation (Chapter 3: Premise 1)— provides the foundation for the creation of communication systems via codification. Recognizing that other people have thoughts and intentions, and being able to treat others' behavior as evidence of those thoughts and intentions, allows people to identify unfamiliar behavior as ostensive. In other words, these abilities allow people to recognize novel sets of social stimuli as potentially being *communicative* in nature (Scott-Phillips, 2015; Scott-Phillips et al., 2009). (For a more extended discussion of recognizing communicative intentions, see Chapter 4). Once that novel set of social stimuli is recognized as potentially communicative, people's capacity for mentalizing also enables them to make inferences about what their interlocutor might be seeking to activate with these stimuli (i.e. what their interlocutor's behavior might "mean").

Through the process of interaction, people are able to test their inferences, and correct or update them accordingly (Clark, 1996; Clark & Brennan, 1991; Clark & Krych, 2004; see also Galantucci, 2005; Healey & Mills, 2006; Healey et al., 2007). This allows communicators to establish that a specific set of stimuli ("X") is intended to activate a particular meme state ("Y"). Once communicators successfully create understanding using a particular set of stimuli, they recognize that this set of stimuli works for this purpose, with this interlocutor. Subsequently, when one of those communicators wants to activate "Y", they make a predictive inference (see Chapter 3: Premise 3) that using "X" will successfully activate "Y", because it has done so before. This leads them to preferentially select "X" as stimuli to present when they want to activate "Y", reinforcing the association between these two elements. With repetition, this association is solidified and routinized.

Galantucci (2005) documented this process in a study in which pairs of participants had to find a way to communicate to complete a task without access to previously established communication systems (e.g. language, kinesics). He observed that under these circumstances, participants first began to identify co-occurrences between each other's behavior and presentation of stimuli (which he termed "signing activity"). Then, participants further probed the potential "meaning" of a stimulus by using the stimulus they had seen a partner use previously, and seeing how the partner reacted. He observed that if this process was used simultaneously by two people who were willing to be adaptive, a basic communication system emerged.

Once an association between a set of stimuli and a meme state is established, we propose that people's predisposition toward efficiency (Chapter 3: Premise 2) prompts a process of formal abstraction over time. Both producing and processing stimuli requires energy. Thus, if people can accomplish the same interactional goal (i.e. activating a given meme state) with less stimuli, and thus less expended energy, a predisposition toward efficiency should lead them to do so. Reducing a stimulus to its essential formal and structural features requires less stimuli, and is thus more efficient in terms of both production and processing (all other things being equal). Given this, there should be a general tendency toward such abstraction over time.

And indeed, in experimental settings where communicators have to develop either novel communication systems or novel references (e.g. labels for objects) to complete a task, there is evidence that communicators move toward more abstracted stimuli (i.e. stimuli that retain a set of essential recognizable features while increasingly omitting details) over a series of trials (e.g. Clark & Krych,

2004; Garrod et al., 2007). Garrod and colleagues (2007) argue that through this process of abstraction, there is a shift in the "locus of information" from the stimulus itself to people's memory of what that stimulus has activated in the history of an interaction. In other words, as meme state activation increasingly draws on the mental associations that communicators have established (and reinforced) through contextualized interaction, the actual stimuli themselves matter less. Instead, interactants only need the stimuli presented to be sufficient to reach a threshold to trigger meme state activation, via their learned associations. Over time, this can be accomplished with fewer, abstracted features.

Experimental evidence from Garrod et al. (2007) suggests that interaction is required to establish what stimulus features are necessary to reach this recognition threshold, and by extension, for the process of formal abstraction to take place. When participants in Garrod et al.'s (2007) study were allowed to interact (in a task that involved communicating via graphical stimuli), the researchers saw the stimuli participants generated simplify across a series of trials. However, when participants were not allowed to interact, and instead were asked to generate stimuli for generic audience, participants' stimuli became increasingly complex across trials. The idea that interaction is necessary for the development of a shared communication system is also consistent with Healey and colleagues' (2007) proposal that convergence on a shared communication system is a result of efforts at interactive repair—that is, providing feedback about the meme state that a given stimulus is supposed to activate when it does not initially function as a communicator intended (see also Healey & Mills, 2006).

Dynamic Stability and Trade-Offs

Through the process we describe here, communication systems can emerge in situations where there was previously no such system. In this, stimuli that were initially used in idiosyncratic ways come to be used more specifically and systematically, and the correspondences between those stimuli and particular meme states are strengthened and narrowed. Over time, the systems that emerge from this process ultimately reach a point of dynamic stability. In other words, after a period of development, communication systems typically reach a stage in which they exhibit a particular degree of codification, and do not become further codified within the same community or set of users. These systems can still change and adapt in their content (e.g. new feature configurations can be created and current feature configurations can fall out of use; associations between feature configurations and memes can shift). For example, in language, new words can be created, "meanings" of words can shift, and terms can become defunct (Crystal,

2006). However, communication systems undergoing such changes retain their overall degree of codification, along the continuum from highly codified to minimally codified described above. Thus, there is not an obligatory, inevitable progression from a low degree of codification to a high degree of codification in communication systems.

This point of dynamic stability in codification varies across communication systems. For example, modern mathematical notation is stable as a highly codified system, as we have described earlier in this chapter. Vocalics, in contrast, is a much less codified system, but is similarly stable in its degree of codification. For centuries, particular intonation patterns, levels of vocal volume, and speech rates (along with a range of other vocal features) have been used by people in a manner similar to their present use. Over that period of time, these feature configurations have not become more highly abstracted in their form, more narrowly associated with specific memes, and more definite (and less probabilistic) in the meme states they evoke.

We propose that the point at which different communication systems stabilize, in terms of codification, is a function of how a system is typically used. More specifically, we propose that a given system's point of dynamic stability is a partial product of optimizing trade-offs between correlates of codification: the consistency of responses to stimuli, context dependence, flexibility of stimuli use, and degree of inference-making and implicature communicators desire or require when using that system. Generally, as consistency of responses increases, context dependence, inference-making, and flexibility in stimuli use decrease.

When people want to activate specific meme states in a highly consistent and unequivocal ways, a system that maximizes consistency of responses and minimizes context dependence and inference-making is ideal. To accomplish these goals, a system sacrifices flexibility in stimuli use; as a result, users of the system generally have to produce more extensive and elaborate sets of stimuli (which requires more energy), because anything they wish to communicate must be made explicit. Engineers, mathematicians, and computer scientists typically want a very high degree of precision in what they communicate to their co-workers, because the stability, operation, and performance of the objects and systems in their work rely on precise inputs. Mathematical notation, one of the primary communication systems used for these functions, has stabilized in a way that serves these purposes well: it is highly codified, and therefore offers a high degree of consistency in responses to stimuli (as manifestations of feature configurations), almost no context dependence, and requires little inference-making. In this system, stimuli have to be used in a very particular and rule-governed manner, and use of stimuli is typically more elaborate. This requires more energy, but this trade-off allows communicators to use it for precision-oriented functions.

In contrast, vocalics offers an example of a communication system that is typically used with different operational goals. Vocalics are typically used in conjunction with spoken language (and often, other systems such as kinesics), and function to augment what is being said verbally. (However, we do note that variation in vocal qualities can sometimes be used on its own). For instance, vocalics can be used to emphasize specific words, convey affect related to what is said, or indicate that an utterance is a question as opposed to a statement. Vocalics can generally achieve these functions with a moderate degree of inference-making and context dependence (particularly when spoken language or another communication system is part of that context). Being able to rely on communicators to draw on other contextual stimuli, and to make more extensive inferences, generally allows communicators to use less stimuli (and to use those stimuli more flexibly) to activate the meme states they intend. This, in turn, can reduce energy expenditure in stimuli production and presentation. As a trade-off, the associations between the feature configurations that communicators use and the meme states activated are less reliable. However, at a system's point of dynamic stability, those (less reliable) associations are typically "good enough" for communicators to accomplish their goals.[4]

In short, we propose that codification in communication systems develops and ultimately stabilizes to be optimized for the way communicators use those systems. Such optimization is consistent with a more general human predisposition toward efficiency (Chapter 3: Premise 2), as it involves using as much energy as is required to accomplish a given goal or function, but not more. The idea that communication systems develop the degree of codification needed for their functional use also parallels our contention that people create understanding—that is, entrain their situation models—to the extent needed for their present purposes (see Chapter 2).

As a final remark on the emergence and development of codification, we want to acknowledge that the codification processes in human communication occur in social and cultural contexts; they also occur through the process of interaction between people, who are biological entities with a distinct evolutionary heritage. As a result, social, biological, and cultural factors influence and potentially constrain the ways in which these systems develop. Some codified systems have roots in our shared evolutionary heritage as humans; others have been constructed within specific social and cultural systems. A discussion of how each of these factors have shaped specific, extant communication systems is beyond the scope and remit of this book, which is to explicate how people create understanding.

However, we do want to underscore that the process of codification is also subject to additional factors we do not fully elaborate here.

Codification and Creating Understanding

Having outlined characteristics and correlates of codification, and discussed how codification develops in communication systems, we now aim to connect these ideas to the central focus of this book: creating understanding. Much of human communication occurs through language, a communication system with a relatively high overall degree of codification. As discussed at the start of this chapter, a focus on language in human communication has predominated in the history of scholarship on human communication, and in interdisciplinary work that relates to understanding (e.g. Clark, 1996; Pickering & Garrod, 2013; Schegloff, 1987; Stephens et al., 2010). Additionally, a "code model" approach to studying communication (see Chapter 1) gives primacy to the shared communication system communicators use to "encode" and "decode" each other's thoughts. These factors have contributed to the implicit notion (and in some cases, assumption) that human communication—and by extension, creating understanding—is dependent on shared, codified systems.

As the model we have presented in Chapter 5 demonstrates, however, codified communication systems are not required for communication, and therefore not required for creating understanding. As described in Chapter 1, one of the major critiques of a "code model" approach to studying communication—which positions codified systems as necessary for communication—is that it cannot address how people manage to successfully create understanding when they improvise in their use of stimuli. Experimental research has demonstrated that people can and do successfully create understanding using instantaneous, flexible conventions— that is, they create understanding using stimuli in novel ways, and using the same stimulus to activate near-opposite meme states in the same interaction (Misyak et al., 2016). This definitively demonstrates that codified systems are not required for creating understanding.

However, codified systems do *facilitate* creating understanding. Knowing that particular feature configurations in stimuli will reliably activate specific meme states allows communicators to select stimuli for specific purposes with greater certainty (using their capacity for predictive inference-making; Chapter 3: Premise 3). It also reduces the need for interaction related to testing, confirming, and/or clarifying the intended effects of communicators' presentation of stimuli (i.e. grounding; Clark & Brennan, 1991). Reducing uncertainty in stimuli selection and reducing the need for interactive confirmation and disambiguation, in turn, reduce the amount of energy communicators need to use to activate their intended meme states. This makes the process of communicating easier, and should allow communicators to create understanding more quickly and more efficiently. Viewed this way, the (preferential) use of codified systems in creating understanding is consistent with humans' predisposition toward efficiency (Chapter 3: Premise 2).

Closely related, we also contend that codified communication systems are a near-inevitable emergent phenomenon following repeated interactions in which communicators share the goal of creating understanding. Put another way, even if people initially seek to create understanding without a codified system, they will almost certainly develop one along the way, if they have opportunities to interact and provide feedback to one another. This emergence of codified systems is a product of basic tendencies in human behavior and cognition (see Chapter 3), as we have just described.

In sum, although human communication does not require codified systems, they play an important role in facilitating the creation of understanding. This helps explain their ubiquity in human communication, despite a lack of necessity. More generally, the theoretical perspective we have presented situates codification within a more general set of observations about human behavior and cognition, and theoretical framework addressing understanding. This, in turn, provides insight into the use, emergence, and varying forms of codified systems observable in human communication, as people create understanding.

Summary

In this chapter, we have advocated for shifting scholarly emphasis in communication research from "codes" as discrete categories and products to codification as descriptive continuum and as a process. We have proposed that reliable associations and formal and structural abstraction are key properties of codification, and provided illustrations of how these properties manifest to different degrees in different communication systems. We have outlined four interrelated correlates of codification that relate to creating understanding—consistency of responses, context dependence, flexibility in stimuli use, and degree of requisite inference-making—and highlighted trade-offs among these correlates. We have also discussed how codified communicative systems develop, arguing that they emerge as a result of human beings' fundamental social orientation, efficiency as a human predisposition, and predictive inference-making as a key feature of human mental activity. Finally, we have argued that codified communication systems facilitate creating understanding by (greatly) increasing the efficiency with which people can activate desired meme states, and thus entrain their situation models.

Notes

1. Burgoon, Guerrero, and Floyd (2010) asked communication scholars to define "nonverbal communication." Although their responses differed in various ways, one distinction that frequently occurred was akin to "any form of communication without words." Such definitions would relegate mathematical and musical notation systems, as well as all forms of aesthetic communication to "nonverbal communication."
2. While this term typically refers to a system with auditory stimuli, we suggest that there is also a visual analog. In written language, punctuation and capitalization function as visual indicators of a codified vocalic communicative system. Commas, semi-colons, periods, ellipses, question marks, exclamation marks are all indicators of vocalic behavior. For example, a person who posts something online in ALL CAPS is often told to "stop shouting."
3. Some scholars have argued that language as a communicative system (i.e. "code") differs qualitatively from other communicative systems (e.g. Scott-Phillips, 2015). We do not dispute that language has properties that differentiate it in important ways from most other systems (e.g. recursivity; a high degree of compositionality combined with very few limits to the topics it can address). Our discussion and comparisons here are only intended to address the degree of codification language exhibits (not necessarily its other properties).
4. We recognize that the examples we have provided focus on retrospectively explaining extant systems. However, with sufficient knowledge of how a new communication system will be used, we believe it should be possible to prospectively predict approximately (although perhaps not exactly) where a new system will stabilize.

References

Birdwhistell, R. L. (1971). *Kinesics and context*. University of Pennsylvania Press. https://doi.org/10.9783/9780812201284

Burgoon, J. K., & Saine, T. (1978). *The unspoken dialogue: An introduction to nonverbal communication*. Houghton Mifflin.

Clark, H. H. (1996). *Using language*. Cambridge University Press. https://doi.org/10.1017/CBO9780511620539

Clark, H. H., & Brennan, S. E. (1991). Grounding in communication. In L. B. Resnick, J. M. Levine, & S. D. Teasley (Eds.), *Perspectives on socially shared cognition*, (pp. 127–149). American Psychological Association. https://doi.org/10.1037/10096-006

Clark, H. H., & Krych, M. A. (2004). Speaking while monitoring addressees for understanding. *Journal of Memory and Language*, *50*(1), 62–81. https://doi.org/10.1016/j.jml.2003.08.004

Crystal, D. (2006). *How language works.* Overlook Press.

Galantucci, B. (2005). An experimental study of the emergence of human communication systems. *Cognitive Science, 29*(5), 737–767. https://doi.org/10.1207/s15516709cog0000_34

Galantucci, B., & Garrod, S. (2011). Experimental semiotics: A review. *Frontiers in Human Neuroscience, 5,* Article 11. https://doi.org/10.3389/fnhum.2011.00011

Galantucci, B., Kroos, C., and Rhodes, T. (2010). The effects of rapidity of fading on communication systems. *Interaction Studies, 11*(1), 100–111. https://doi.org/10.1075/is.11.1.03gal

Garrod, S., Fay, N., Lee, J., Oberlander, J., and MacLeod, T. (2007). Foundations of representation: Where might graphical symbol systems come from? *Cognitive Science, 31*(6), 961–987. https://doi.org/10.1080/03640210701703659

Goldin-Meadow, S., & Feldman, H. (1977). The development of language-like communication without a language model. *Science, 197*(4301), 401–403. https://doi.org/10.1126/science.877567

Goldin-Meadow, S., & Mylander, C. (1998). Spontaneous sign systems created by deaf children in two cultures. *Nature, 391*(6664), 279–281. https://doi.org/10.1038/34646

Hall, E. (1966). *The hidden dimension.* Doubleday.

Healey, P. G., & Mills, G. (2006). Participation, precedence and co-ordination in dialogue. In *Proceedings of the 28th Annual Conference of the Cognitive Science Society* (Vol. 320). Erlbaum.

Healey, P. G. T., Swoboda, N., Umata, I., and King, J. (2007). Graphical language games: Interactional constraints on representational form. *Cognitive Science, 31*(2), 285–309. https://doi.org/10.1080/15326900701221363

McCallum, K., Mitchell, S. & Scott-Phillips, T. (2020). The art experience. *Review of Philosophy and Psychology, 11,* 21–35. https://doi.org/10.1007/s13164-019-00443-y

Misyak, J., Noguchi, T., & Chater, N. (2016). Instantaneous conventions: The emergence of flexible communicative signals. *Psychological Science, 27*(12), 1550–1561. https://doi.org/10.1177/0956797616661199

Pereltsvaig, A. (2012). *Languages of the world: An introduction.* Cambridge University Press. https://doi.org/10.1017/CBO9781139026178

Piantadosi, S. T., Tily, H., & Gibson, E. (2012). The communicative function of ambiguity in language. *Cognition, 122*(3), 280–291. https://doi.org/10.1016/j.cognition.2011.10.004

Pickering, M. J., & Garrod, S. (2013). An integrated theory of language production and comprehension. *Behavioral and Brain Sciences, 36*(4), 329–347. https://doi.org/10.1017/S0140525X12001495

Ramsey, S. J., (1976). Prison codes. *Journal of Communication, 26*(3), 39–45. https://doi.org/10.1111/j.1460-2466.1976.tb01901.x

Reboul, A. C. (2015). Why language really is not a communication system: A cognitive view of language evolution. *Frontiers in Psychology, 6,* Article 1434. https://doi.org/10.3389/fpsyg.2015.01434

Schegloff, E. A. (1987). Some sources of misunderstanding in talk in interaction. *Linguistics, 25,* 201–218. https://doi.org/10.1515/ling.1987.25.1.201

Scott-Phillips, T. C. (2015). *Speaking our minds: Why human communication is different, and how language evolved to make it special*. Palgrave Macmillan.

Scott-Phillips, T. C., Kirby, S., and Ritchie, G. R. S. (2009). Signalling signalhood and the emergence of communication. *Cognition, 113*(2), 226–233. https://doi.org/10.1016/j.cognition.2009.08.009

Shannon, C. E., & Weaver, W. (1949). *The mathematical theory of communication.* University of Illinois Press.

Smith, K., Kirby, S., & Brighton, H. (2003). Iterated learning: A framework for the emergence of language. *Artificial Life, 9*(4), 371–386. https://doi.org/10.1162/106454603322694825

Stephens, G. J., Silbert, L. J., & Hasson, U. (2010). Speaker-listener neural coupling underlies successful communication. *Proceedings of the National Academy of Sciences, 107*, 14425–14430. https://doi.org/10.1073/pnas.1008662107

Theisen, C. A., Oberlander, J., and Kirby, S. (2010). Systematicity and arbitrariness in novel communication systems. *Interaction Studies, 11*, 14–32. https://doi.org/10.1075/is.11.1.08the

Tomasello, M. (2008). *Origins of human communication*. Jean-Nicod lectures. MIT Press. https://doi.org/10.7551/mitpress/7551.001.0001

Vinciarelli, A., Pantic, M., Magnenat-Thalmann, N., & Burgoon, J. (Eds.). (2017). *Social signal processing*. Cambridge University Press.

Wiener, M., Devoe, S., Rubinow, S., & Geller, J. (1972). Nonverbal behavior and nonverbal communication. *Psychological Review, 79*, 185–214. https://doi.org/10.1037/h0032710

CHAPTER EIGHT

Connections and Implications

This chapter discusses how the perspective and model we have introduced complement and connect to a selection of other, extant theories in the discipline of communication. Specifically, we address links to theorizing on adjustment and adaptation in communication, entrainment, expectations and uncertainty, deception, and intercultural and intergroup communication. In this, we underscore the ways in which our framework offers an additional explanatory dimension to traditional concepts and theories in the discipline. We also discuss the theoretical and methodological implications of the conceptualizations, model, and perspective on understanding we have proposed.

The perspective and process model we have proposed in the preceding chapters draw on theoretical and empirical work on communication and understanding from a variety of sources, most of which are outside the discipline of communication. However, we believe the framework we have outlined can both complement and extend other theories in the discipline of communication that address related topics (but do not address understanding focally). In this chapter, we provide examples of some of these potential connections for a selection of theories, and then discuss the theoretical and methodological implications of acknowledging and prioritizing a focus on understanding in communication scholarship.

Adjustment and Adaptation in Communication

Many theories of communication and its effects highlight the importance of adapting or adjusting messages for one's audience (for a review of theories of interpersonal adjustment, see Gasiorek, 2016). For example, constructivism argues that using messages that are tailored to a specific individual in context should be more effective at achieving communicators' goals, broadly defined, than messages that are not (e.g. Delia, 1977; Gastil, 1995). Definitions and theorizing on (intercultural) communication competence emphasize the importance of adapting messages so they are appropriate to the cultural and relational context (e.g. Imahori & Lanigan, 1989; Kim, 2005; Pitts & Harwood, 2015; Spitzberg, 1983). Communication accommodation theory (CAT), an expansive theoretical framework that aims to explain and predict communicative adjustment in context, argues that adapting communicative behavior is a primary means by which people accomplish their interactional goals (Giles, 2016; Pitts & Harwood, 2015; Zhang & Giles, 2018). In this, CAT proposes that accommodating one's communication in context serves two primary functions: managing understanding and managing social relationships (Dragojevic et al., 2016).

The framework we have proposed complements and augments these frameworks by offering a cognitive explanation for *how* adapting messages for one's audience is important to accomplishing communicators' goals. Constructivism has been critiqued for its relatively shallow explanations of the theoretical relationships it proposes, and for its lack of attention to cognitive mediators (Gastil, 1995). Scholarship on communication competence generally suggests that adjustment is important, but does not specify the process by which adjustment will lead to better outcomes. To date, both empirical and theoretical work using CAT has focused primarily on motivations for, and effects of, communicative adjustment as they relate to social relationships (Soliz & Giles, 2014). How communication adjustment allows people to manage understanding has received comparatively little theoretical attention.

Our framework helps address these gaps by specifying a process by which adjustment leads to more effective communication. Restated in our terminology, a message that accommodates its audience is essentially a set of stimuli that are selected in a way that accounts for the cognitive characteristics of its target, as well as the immediate context. We have proposed that stimuli initially activate the meme state that is most accessible to a communicator, and that communicators exert greater effort (and more processing cycles) if this initial meme state is not consistent with their situation model's predictions. If people select social stimuli that account for both the immediate context and their interlocutor's existing situation model, this should improve the (relative) accessibility of communicators' desired meme state for that interlocutor. This, in turn, should make that particular meme state more likely to be the initial meme state that is activated (or a meme state activated early in iterative attempts at addressing discrepancies). To the extent that activating specific meme states allows communicators to accomplish their goals, stimuli selection that is adapted to a specific situation should be more effective at doing so.

This additional detail in explaining the process by which adjustment relates to effective communication has theoretical and empirical implications. First, our framework suggests that adjustment may not just be helpful or beneficial; rather, it may be essential to accomplishing communicators' goals. We theorize that the accessibility of (desired) meme states is a function of both the immediate context and a given communicator's mental structures (which, in turn, are shaped by that person's background). Viewed this way, activating a desired meme state *requires* adapting stimuli selection to account for interlocutors' current and anticipated mental structures and mental representations; there is no generic or "one size fits all" solution to selecting stimuli that will be optimally accessible. Additionally, and related, the process we specify could allow for more precise predictions (or retrospective explanation or diagnosis) of the effects of specific types of adjustments than current frameworks offer, if researchers have sufficient knowledge of communicators' previous mental models (e.g. knowledge, past experience).

Entrainment

A number of theories and constructs in interpersonal communication research also note or highlight humans' tendencies toward synchrony, alignment, and/or entrainment (e.g. Burgoon et al., 2017). For example, early work using CAT focused on (linguistic) *convergence*, the tendency for people's communicative behavior to become more similar to that of their interlocutors. The explanation for this phenomenon provided by CAT focused on social factors, arguing that people often converged in their communication behavior to pursue or highlight shared social identity (Dragojevic et al., 2016). Interaction adaption theory (IAT) argues that people have a basic (biological) tendency toward synchrony and entrainment, but that personal and situational factors moderate these needs, and how they manifest in communication (Burgoon & Ebesu Hubbard, 2005). Research on mimicry has demonstrated that people unconsciously mirror each other's behavior in interaction (Chartrand & van Baaren, 2009). Additionally, research on language style matching (LSM; Ireland & Pennebaker, 2010; Niederhoffer & Pennebaker,

2002) demonstrates that people also engage in verbal synchronization in their use of function words (e.g. articles, conjunctions, auxiliary verbs, prepositions), outside of conscious awareness. Interactants' degree of LSM has been correlated with their level of engagement in conversation (Niederhoffer & Pennebaker, 2002), and LSM researchers have proposed that this type of coordination may help people align their mental frameworks in ways that enable and facilitate interaction (Ireland & Pennebaker, 2010).

The framework we have proposed offers several complementary insights and extensions to this body of work. First and most importantly, extant research on communication and variants on synchrony has focused on *behavioral* entrainment. We explicitly extend and connect these varied observations about synchrony in behavior to synchrony in *cognitive* experiences—that is, to entrainment of mental models (for similar arguments, see Hasson & Frith, 2016; Shamay-Tsoory et al., 2019). Through our conceptualization of *understanding* as a state of entrained situation models, we also connect scholarship on entrainment in communicative behavior to understanding, a topic that several of the constructs and theories we note (i.e. IAT, mimicry, LSM) do not explicitly address.

Second, we also offer a link between these observations on behavior and cognition and recent neuroscientific research demonstrating that when people successfully create understanding, they experience coupling, or entrainment, of brain activity (e.g. Hasson et al., 2012; Stephens et al., 2010). This extends extant theorizing in the discipline by offering linkages across behavior, cognition, and neural activity. The presence of such connections is consistent with previous theorizing outside of the discipline of communication, such as Pickering and Garrod's (2004) interactive alignment model, that make compelling arguments for "vertical" links between behavior and levels of cognition.

Third, our model also positions *predictive* processes as central to entrainment and social coordination in a way that most of the constructs and theories noted above do not. (We do, however, note that predictive processes are acknowledged in other, extant frameworks outside the discipline of communication that address entrainment; for example, Pickering & Garrod, 2013). This offers an additional theoretical dimension to both explaining and predicting synchrony and entrainment in interaction, and outcomes related to it.

Connections to our framework also permit some predictions about conditions under which we might observe greater behavioral entrainment. As we have discussed in previous chapters, extant research connects quantitative measures of comprehension to (anticipatory) neural coupling. In our framework, understanding is conceptualized as alignment or entrainment of communicators' situation models, which are both descriptive and predictive mental structures. Following from this, we propose that we should likely see higher levels of behavioral entrainment (e.g. LSM, behavioral mimicry) when communicators experience higher degrees of (a) entrainment in their situation models, (b) neural coupling, or entrainment, and perhaps also (c) subjective understanding. Entrainment of situation models could be operaticnalized in questions addressing both the content and nature of the interaction at a given point in time (either at a point where participants are stopped and asked, or in procedures like video-assisted recall); it could also be operationalized as anticipation or prediction of what would occur next in the interaction. As we consider predictions to be an important components of communicators' situation models, we also suggest that operationalizations of entrainment or alignment that focus on communicators' predictions of what will occur next (as opposed to the present state of the interaction) might be more highly correlated with behavioral entrainment or synchrony.

Finally, with respect to CAT specifically, our framework offers a potential explanation for why linguistic convergence—that is, increasing similarity in communication style—can facilitate understanding. We propose that when communicators use the same stimuli (e.g. words, structures, or pronunciations) as their interlocutors, they are essentially taking advantage of patterns of activation and/or associations between stimuli and meme states that have been previously established in the interaction (via their interlocutors' usage). This, in turn, should facilitate entrainment of meme states and situation models. As discussed in the Chapter 7, the tendency for communicators to (re)use the same stimuli as one another to activate specific meme states also contributes to the development of codified communication systems. Thus, our framework also offers (to the best of our knowledge) novel links between processes theorized in CAT and the more general process of codification in human communication.

Expectations and Uncertainty

Several extant communication theories discuss or reference the importance of expectations to interaction, and discuss the effects that unexpected (communicative) behavior can have. For example, CAT posits that people's expectations about their interlocutors (which can follow from interpersonal or intergroup history, as well as perceptions of communicators' characteristics) are a part of their *initial orientation* in an interaction, and affect how people choose to accommodate their communication (Dragojevic et al., 2016). Similarly, self-categorization theory (SCT) argues that people's expectations about individuals they encounter—which are theorized to follow from stereotypes activated by the social categorization processes—affect how people behave in interaction (Turner et al., 1987). Expectancy violations theory (EVT) addresses how people respond when others act in ways that are inconsistent with their expectancies, focusing on the valence of people's reactions (while acknowledging attendant outcomes for the nature of the interaction) (Burgoon, 1993). EVT posits that discrepancies between expectations and reality lead to psychological arousal, arguing that this arousal draws attention to the discrepancy.

There is also a conceptually related (but often, theoretically and empirically distinct) body of communication scholarship addressing uncertainty. Uncertainty reduction theory, an early framework in this area, argued that "when strangers meet, their primary concern is one of uncertainty reduction or increasing predictability about the behavior of both themselves and others in the interaction" (Berger & Calabrese, 1975, p. 100). In subsequent decades, communication researchers expanded their focus beyond initial interactions, and observed that there are situations in which people may prefer to remain uncertain (e.g. when uncertainty offers hope; Brashers, 2001). In line with this, more recent theories like uncertainty management theory (UMT; Brashers, 2001) and the theory of motivated information management (TMIM; Afifi & Weiner, 2004) have contended that people actively manage their uncertainty about issues that are important to them, and do so via interpersonal communication.

Prediction, we propose, is a common thread across theorizing on both expectations and uncertainty. Prediction is implicit in the notion of expectations: expectations are essentially predictive inferences about what will happen in a given contextualized interaction. Prediction is also implicated in uncertainty: reducing uncertainty corresponds to increasing predictability regarding a given future outcome (e.g. what a person will do next; Berger & Calabrese, 1975), and vice versa. The theories we have summarized here generally address prediction (via expectations or uncertainty) as it relates to communicators' social, relational, or informational goals. Our framework complements and extends this work, arguing that prediction plays an important role at another, more basic level: we position predictive inference-making as a fundamental mechanism in human mental activity (Chapter 3: Premise 3).

In so doing, we propose a (shared) foundation for theorizing about both expectations and uncertainty. In this, we offer an explanation grounded in theorizing on human evolution for why prediction is important, and therefore a fundamental consideration in the way people approach the world (see Chapter 3). In other chapters, we have also highlighted links to recent neuroscientific literature that demonstrate that prediction is a feature of human brain (i.e. neural) activity, as well as cognition in successful communication (e.g. Stephens et al., 2010).

This offers a physiological foundation for the central role of prediction in inter-action—and thus, by extension, both expectations and uncertainty management. Our perspective thus roots communication theories that focus on expectations, uncertainty, and predictability in broader and more generalized foundations.

We also connect expectations and uncertainty management (via prediction) to the process of creating understanding specifically; this complements other extant frameworks, which focus on affective reactions and/or other communica-tive behavior as outcomes. In our framework, we articulate a theoretical role for expectations in communication processes that is both more specific and somewhat different than some other theories. Similar to EVT, we position generating pre-dictions and testing those predictions against reality as the core mental process in human communication. However, as discussed in the previous section, we argue that this is something people do (specifically) in pursuit of entraining their situa-tion models with their interlocutors'. Following from this, we suggest that in the context of communication, it may not necessarily be the violation of expectations itself that is experienced as cognitively problematic (leading to arousal). Rather, it may be recognizing a lack of entrainment (via prediction error, or discrepancies between expectations and reality) that is arousing. This implicit recognition may then be what motivates communicators to devote additional mental resources to (re-)establishing entrainment, by resolving discrepancies between their previous expectations and reality.

Our process model can also be applied to explain how people engage in uncertainty management, offering a different perspective on how the outcomes predicted by UMT and the TMIM manifest in cognition. Specifically, we sug-gest that uncertainty management (in interaction) can be viewed as a process of strategic entrainment of specific dimensions of situation models. As we have described, situation models are multidimensional, and communicators entrain particular dimensions of their situation models (only) to the extent needed for their current purposes, often in ways that are goal-driven. Thus, we offer a novel way to conceptualize uncertainty management: as creating understanding in a calculated and controlled manner.

Finally, our framework also provides additional detail on how expectations shape subsequent interaction, as proposed in frameworks like CAT or SCT. Through the lens of our framework, expectations related to the communicative context (e.g. communicator characteristics, stereotypes, interpersonal or inter-group history) can be seen as dimensions of communicators' initial situation model that are activated by contextual stimuli. According to our model, as components of situation models—which are both descriptive and predictive—these expecta-tions subsequently inform predictions for what will happen next in interaction.

We theorize that these predictions affect how people process and respond to the social stimuli their interlocutors present; specifically, the meme states activated and the situation models constructed through the process we have outlined are what guide behavior in interaction. Thus, we offer a model of the cognitive process through which the links between expectations and behavior posited by theories like CAT and SCT occur.

Deception

The study of deception is an increasingly well-developed subdiscipline of social scientific communication research (e.g. Knapp et al., 2020). Key observations in contemporary deception research include that deception is defined by deceptive intent, and that deceptive messages can take a variety of different forms: in addition to outright (or "bald-faced") lies, it can include omission, evasion, and misleading statements composed of truthful information (Knapp et al., 2020; Levine, 2014). Several theories offer explanations and predictions of how deception is enacted, and how people process deceptive messages. For example, information manipulation theory 2 (IMT2; McCornack et al., 2014) proposes that communicators will produce different types of deceptive messages under different conditions, and that these differences are guided by the amount of effort required to produce different sorts of messages in context. Truth-default theory (TDT; Levine, 2014) addresses how people process deceptive messages; as the name suggests, it proposes that people's default assumption is that their interlocutors are honest in their communication. TDT argues that this is adaptive, and promotes efficient communication (Levine, 2014; see also Dennett, 2017).

The framework we have proposed offers a general process model that contributes to explanations of deceptive communication in ways that are consistent with both IMT2 and TDT. Like IMT2, we argue that efficiency (akin to IMT2's "least effort") is a guiding principle that affects both what stimuli communicators will select to accomplish their goals (i.e. what form their deceptive messages will take), and how they will process that stimuli (i.e. what meme states will be activated in response to the stimuli presented). As IMT2 outlines, this helps explain why communicators may choose different stimuli (i.e. use different forms of deceptive messages) in different circumstances. Our process model, and conceptualizations of communication and creating understanding, also allow us to parsimoniously explain how various forms of deception function. We suggest that different forms of deception (e.g. omission, evasion, misleading statements) all operate in essentially the same manner: communicators use stimuli that activate meme states, and this process contributes to the construction of situation models. This is generally consistent with IMT2's explanation of deception as "manipulation of information" (McCornack et al. 2014). However, we offer greater specificity on how communicators enact this manipulation: we propose that communicators select stimuli based on predictive inferences about what these stimuli will likely activate for their interlocutors. Through this, they strategically entrain specific dimensions of their situation models with their interlocutors'.

The framework we present also provides some additional insights into how people recognize deceptive intent as third parties. In most cases, the process of meme state activation that follows from a particular set of stimuli is likely to be somewhat generalizable within a communicative community. This suggests that, in the case of deception, others who witness or hear about a deceptive exchange will likely recognize that they too would have experienced the same meme states and/or situation model as the deceived person if they had been presented with those stimuli, in context This recognition of generalizability (in combination with people's more general capacity for mentalizing), in turn, allows people to attribute deceptive intent to that communicator.

Given this, it follows from our framework that the most successful deceptions must strike a balance between how well stimuli activate desired meme states relative to how widespread that activation process is within a communicative community. That is, if deceivers wish to "get away with" their deception, or at worst be seen only as party to a misunderstanding, they have to maximize the likelihood of activating their desired meme states while minimizing the extent to which other communicators, or other parties directly or indirectly engaged in the communicative event, can attribute intentionality to that activation process.

In short, we propose that deception can be seen as a special case of creating understanding. Just like truthful communication, deception is a situation in which communicators have the goal of activating particular meme states, and by extension cultivating particular situation models, in their interlocutors' minds (see Chapter 6). The crucial difference is that in deceptive communication, the meme states that one communicator seeks to activate differ from what that communicator knows to be true. As such, a deceptive communicator's goal is selective, partial entrainment of situation models, rather than the broader entrainment (to the degree required by their needs) that communicators pursue in truthful communication. Further, the deceiver's goal of creating selective entrainment remains covert, consistent with conceptualizations of deception in IMT2. Thus, our framework provides a theoretical link between deception and understanding, and potentially offers an alternative way to think about the process of deception.

Communicative Challenges in Intercultural and Intergroup Communication

Finally, it is widely observed that intercultural and intergroup communication are often experienced as more challenging than intracultural or intragroup communication. What is labeled "miscommunication" or "misunderstanding"—that is, interactions in which communicators do not entrain their situation models sufficiently for their current purposes—tends to occur more frequently in such situations (e.g. Korkut et al., 2018). Communicators also tend to experience intercultural or intergroup interactions as less fluent, more effortful, and therefore more difficult.

The framework we propose helps explain why people experience intercultural and intergroup communication as more difficult, and why issues with understanding can be more frequent in these types of interactions. As already discussed, we posit that processing effort plays an important role in meme state activation. The processing effort required to activate a given meme state, for a given stimulus, in turn, is affected by people's previous experiences (see Chapter 4). Both culture and social identity are important factors that shape these experiences (which, we also note, are ongoing: any communicative experiences people have become "previous experiences" for their next interaction; Dragojevic et al., 2016).

As we have discussed in Chapter 6, when communicators are from the same social group or culture, they are likely to share some similar past experiences of meme state activation. As a result, they are likely to experience similar responses to a given set of stimuli. Thus, when communicators interact with ingroup members, members of their own culture, and people with similar past experiences (with respect to content related to that shared background, group membership, culture, or set of experiences), selecting stimuli that correspond to communicators' own patterns of meme state activation should be reasonably effective at activating their desired meme states for others.

We suggest that, in general, people's default tendency is to provide others with stimuli that correspond to their own patterns of meme state activation, unless they have specific knowledge about their audience that prompts them to do otherwise. (Similar observations have been made about perspective-taking more generally; for example, Epley et al., 2004). For example, people from the United States typically use the term "trunk" to refer to the storage space typically found in the rear of a car, while people from the United Kingdom use "boot". Speakers of each variety of English generally use their own default term unless they are consciously aware, at the moment of formulating these stimuli, that their interlocutor does not speak their variety of English. We propose that this occurs because it is an efficient choice (Chapter 3: Premise 2) in the absence of knowledge about potential differences between oneself and one's interlocutor. As an efficient choice, it also feels "easy", or fluent, for communicators to select their own default stimuli. (We note that these observations, grounded in our model, may help explain people's tendencies toward ethnocentrism in communicative choices).

If communicators have similar previous experiences of meme state activation (following from a shared culture or ingroup), their own default stimuli should readily and effectively activate the meme states they intend. However, when communicators are from different social groups or cultures, they are less likely to share some similar past experiences of meme state activation. If communicators do not have these similar experiences, one communicator's default use of stimuli may activate unintended meme states for their interlocutors (e.g. "boot" activating "ankle-covering footwear"). This can be avoided in (at least) two possible ways. First, communicators presenting stimuli can override their default stimuli selection, and offer stimuli that are deliberately adapted for their interlocutor, if they have the requisite knowledge to do so (e.g. a British English speaker substituting "trunk" for "boot" for an American interlocutor). Second, communicators processing stimuli can recognize that the meme state activated does not make sense in context, and they can (a) search for an alternative meme state the stimuli could conceivably activate in context, (b) modify their situation model for the interaction, or (c) seek out additional stimuli to disambiguate, as described in Chapter 4. In all cases, the alternative route requires more energy and effort by communicators. As such, interactions in which this occurs may subjectively feel more difficult or disfluent.

This explanation also offers some insight into why misunderstanding is more frequent in intercultural or intergroup interactions. Because communicators from different social or cultural groups are less likely to share similar past experiences of meme state activation (and related associations between stimuli and meme states), there is generally a greater need for adaptation or compensation in stimuli selection and activation to create understanding successfully. If communicators do not recognize this need, there is a higher likelihood they will select stimuli and experience meme state activations that do not correspond to each other's situation models (e.g. Hewett et al., 2015). As described in our framework, when this occurs, it results in either (a) the need for additional effort—and potentially, interaction—to address these issues and bring their situation models in line, or (b) misunderstanding (i.e. a lack of sufficient entrainment in situation models) between communicators. The latter is especially likely if insufficient entrainment is not recognized, and/or attempts to address it are unsuccessful.

In short, our framework offers a functional explanation for challenges related to communication and/or understanding in intercultural and intergroup encounters. At present, a dominant approach to addressing intercultural communication competence is to focus on increasing knowledge and awareness of other cultures' practices (e.g. Baker et al., 2017; Kim, 2005). This work is often grounded in research on cross-cultural comparisons, which highlight differences in values, behavior and communicative practices between members of different cultures (Kim, 2005). This approach clearly recognizes that communicative challenges exist, but it does not necessarily address *why* they exist, beyond fairly proximal causes. The framework we propose complements this work by offering a theoretical foundation upon which such observations, and corresponding education and interventions, could be based.

Theoretical Implications

In addition to the points of connection with current communication scholarship we have just outlined, the content of our framework also has a number of theoretical implications for scholarship in the discipline. In what follows, we briefly outline some of these implications.

First, conceptualizing understanding as a state of entrainment augments conventional notions of communication as a means of social "connection". Traditionally, this kind of terminology, and the concept it implies, has primarily been loose and metaphorical. However, conceptualizing understanding as a state in which people's mental representations and corresponding brain activity become entrained offers an additional dimension to the idea of *connection*. That is, when people successfully create understanding (via communication), they experience a physiological connection in the form of coupled neural activity.

From this, it follows that a dyad (or group) that successfully creates understanding can (temporarily) be seen as a single or integrated system. We think this has potentially interesting implications for theorizing about phenomena like groupthink, as well as the social effects of communication (e.g. perceptions of affiliation or social distance; the role of communication in building relationships; Aune & Aune, 2019). For example, social penetration theory (Taylor & Altman, 1987) argues for the importance of disclosure in building relationships; this argument is built on an implicit assumption that relational development is an informational process of people learning about one other. The perspective we offer suggests there may also be additional dimension to the value of disclosure: experiences of creating understanding as manifested in neural entrainment offer people experiences of physiological connection that might produce greater perceptions of closeness (e.g. Morelli et al., 2014). Whether this is the case is ultimately an empirical question, of course.

Second, and closely related, our framework offers a potentially novel perspective on the nature of asynchronous communication. In most of this book, we have focused on synchronous (and face-to-face) communication as a prototypical interaction. However, the conceptualization of understanding and the basic model we have proposed apply and function equally well for asynchronous encounters (with some potential differences in how communicators engage in disambiguation and error correction; see Chapter 6). In all cases, according to our model, understanding is successfully achieved when communicators' situation models are entrained. However, in asynchronous contexts, this entrainment occurs with a time lag: that is, we expect alignment of situation models to occur relative to a given point in the set of stimuli created or presented. For example, we would say readers "understand" a written text when their situation models at a given point in a text align with the situation model the writer had in mind when writing that section of text (to the extent necessary for readers' purposes). This implies that reading a text, or listening to a story or piece of music, allows people to reconstruct and experience (to at least some extent) the mental states of others that are physically and temporally distant. Reading Shakespeare's plays allows people to temporarily experience mental states that Shakespeare himself experienced—down to the level of neural activity—across a gap of over 400 years. It is widely observed that communication—and particularly, language—allows people to share ideas across time and space (e.g. Crystal, 2006). However, we believe that our conceptualization of understanding as entrainment offers an additional dimension to, as well as a somewhat novel perspective on, this observation.

A third implication of our framework is that traditional divisions between "verbal" and "nonverbal" communication may not be theoretically useful for addressing how human communication functions. Our model offers an explanation of how people communicate, and create understanding, in which all forms of stimuli essentially function in the same way: they activate meme states and contribute to constructing and updating situation models. When the process of communication is viewed this way, there is not a need to create a distinction between verbal and nonverbal "forms" of communication, because they are not functionally distinct. Closely related, in contrast to much of previous scholarship on both communication and understanding (within and outside the discipline of communication), we do not give language a privileged position in our theorizing. We absolutely recognize that language is a powerful and important tool for human communication; we also acknowledge that it may differ qualitatively from other codified systems that people use to communicate (Scott-Phillips, 2015). However, in terms of the actual *process* of communicating and creating understanding, our framework posits that language functions similarly to other forms of stimuli.

Fourth and finally, considering the neurological substrates of communication and creating understanding also highlights that each interaction people experience is a neurological event that potentially leaves physiological traces. In *transactional* models of communication, interpersonal scholars have argued that every communicative event affects its interactants, leaving them "changed" (Barnlund, 1970). Our framework is consistent with this observation, but suggests this is not just metaphorical; it is also physical. Meme state activation is a biological event; each time a meme state is activated (via social or contextual stimuli), the brain undergoes a physical change. The same can be argued for constructing, updating, and entraining situation models. We have proposed that previous experiences of meme state activation, as well as extant situation models, affect what meme states are activated in response to stimuli. More specifically, previously established associations and frequent or recent activation of particular meme states should make those meme states—and corresponding situation models—more readily accessible (see Chapter 4). This suggests that every interaction in which entrainment is approximated or achieved restructures the neural patterns of activation to some degree (Aune & Aune, 2019). These considerations potentially offer a novel way of thinking about the traditional notion that communication "transforms" or "changes" people.

Methodological Implications

The framework we have proposed also has methodological implications for studying understanding, as well as communication more generally. As there is relatively little research in the discipline of communication on understanding itself, we first address methodological implications for the study of communication in more general terms. We then offer suggestions for how researchers can approach studying understanding.

As we discussed in Chapter 1, to date, a majority of research studies looking at human communication have been designed to examine the thoughts and behaviors of one person at a time. When researchers are interested in message construction, they focus on the thoughts and actions of the message "source" or "sender". When researchers are interested in message effects, they focus on the thoughts and actions of the message "receiver", "audience", or "target". In such studies, the researchers' unit of analysis is the individual.

This tendency to focus on the individual may be an artifact of the evolution of the field of communication, particularly its roots in rhetoric and oratory, as well as the more recent history of research focused on mass communication. Since these communicative situations are characterized by communicators in clearly defined and relatively static roles as senders or receivers (often with limited feedback between them), it is reasonable to focus on one role (i.e. "sending" or "receiving"), and therefore one communicator, at a time. (We also venture that the dominance of this approach in the discipline of communication may have inadvertently biased researchers away from studying understanding, which is inherently dyadic).

It is also worth noting that studies using this traditional approach are relatively straightforward to carry out, as participants may be recruited and scheduled individually. Additionally, as noted in Chapter 1, traditional inferential statistics—which is what most quantitative communication scholars are taught in their undergraduate and graduate training—address individuals as the unit of analysis, and assume independence of observations. Scholarly work using this *monologic* approach has certainly contributed to our knowledge of how communication works. However, it offers limited insight into communication as a dynamic, interactional process.

Although more or less all theoretical models of human communication depict communication as a dyadic (and interactive) phenomenon, a minority of extant research studies in communication employ a *dialogic* approach to also study it as such. This is likely because of the increased difficulty and complexity of conducting such studies, in terms of both data collection (e.g. requiring the coordination of multiple participants) and data analysis (e.g. requiring statistical analysis that account for interdependence, or techniques to code and analyze recordings of interactions, which can be time- and labor-intensive). Additionally, as noted above, many of the contexts in which researchers have traditionally studied "communication" have been fairly asynchronous and minimally reciprocal. However, if researchers wish to study communication in synchronous and reciprocal interactive contexts, it is not reasonable or appropriate to examine communicators independently, because their behavior and cognitions are interdependent (Schilbach, et al., 2013). This, we argue, extends to studying understanding.

The framework we have proposed conceptualizes understanding as a state of entrainment, which is an inherently dyadic phenomenon, defined by interdependence. As such, it is not possible to theorize or measure entrainment of a single, independent unit on its own. If researchers wish to focus on one unit in a system characterized by entrainment, they may do so, but they still need to address what their focal unit is entrained with. From this, it follows that studying understanding essentially requires a dialogic approach (e.g. Garrod & Pickering, 2004; Hari & Kujala, 2009; Hasson, et al., 2012; Pickering & Garrod, 2004). If researchers would like to determine whether communicators have successfully created understanding, they need to measure or otherwise assess (e.g. via behavioral proxies) the cognitions of all communicators involved in a communicative episode.

Ideally, such studies should incorporate designs that employ dyadic (or group) data collection and analysis. Such designs allow researchers to examine interaction as a dynamic process, which is important for examining issues like how people engage in interactive disambiguation and error correction in the process of creating understanding (e.g. Clark & Krych, 2004). Arguably, studies of dyadic or group interactions also offer a higher level of ecological validity. As Garrod and Pickering (2004) have noted, most of people's communicative interactions are dialogues (i.e. conversations). To the extent that researchers can study understanding in a way that reflects this, they will have a better and more accurate picture of this phenomenon as it occurs in the real world.

With that said, we recognize the methodological challenges that dyadic (or group) data analysis and collection entail. We believe that with thoughtful study designs, it is possible to study understanding with individual participants. As discussed above, we contend that the experience of understanding (as a state of entrainment), and the core process by which people create understanding, is the same in synchronous and asynchronous contexts. Thus, researchers can create communicative scenarios where communicators present and process stimuli during different sessions. (For researchers interested in studying codification, these sessions can be chained across time, as in iterated learning designs; for example, Smith et al., 2003). Researchers could also examine subcomponents of the process by which people create understanding (as we have proposed it) with individual participants. For example, the sub-process of meme state activation (theorized as a potentially iterative process of comparison between situation model predictions and meme states activated according to accessibility) is an individual-level phenomenon that could be studied using more traditional approaches.

In all of these cases, however, we argue that it is critical to maintain a dialogic approach to operationalizing understanding. Specifically, data between communicators needs to be linked, and analyzed as such, even if it is collected at different points in time. If the researcher essentially functions as one of the communicators in the dyad—for example, by designing stimuli with a specific situation model in mind—the content of that situation model needs to be an explicit part of the study's design. If the study addresses understanding, the degree of correspondence between participants' situation models and the researcher's situation model should be a focus of data collection and analysis. Our framework highlights that even when research designs allowing individual participants are tenable, assessing whether communicators have successfully created understanding is inherently and unavoidably dyadic. In the next chapter, we provide suggestions and potential examples of what empirical work using such an approach could look like.

Summary

In this chapter, we have discussed how the framework we have proposed complements and potentially augments theorizing on human communication in a selection of areas: adjustment and adaptation in communication, entrainment, expectations and uncertainty, deception, and challenges in intercultural and intergroup communication. We have also discussed the theoretical implications of our framework for traditional notions of communication and "social connection", asynchronous communication, divisions between "verbal" and "nonverbal" communication, and the effects of communication on interactants. Finally, we have also discussed the methodological implications of our conceptualization of understanding, advocating the importance of a dialogic approach to studying this phenomenon.

References

Afifi, W. A., & Weiner, J. L. (2004). Toward a theory of motivated information management. *Communication Theory, 14*(2), 167–190. https://doi.org/10.1111/j.1468-2885.2004.tb00310.x

Aune, K. S., & Aune, R. K. (2019). Entraining, becoming, and loving. In R. J. Sternberg & K. Sternberg (Eds.). *New psychology of love (2nd ed.)* (pp. 25–41). Cambridge University Press. https://doi.org/10.1017/9781108658225.003

Baker, S., Watson, B. M., & Gallois, C. (2017). Exploring intercultural communication problems in health care with a communication accommodation competence approach. In L. Chen (Ed.), *Intercultural communication,* Volume 9 of *Handbooks of communication science* (pp. 481–499). Mouton de Gruyter. https://doi.org/10.1515/9781501500060-022

Barnlund, D. C. (1970). A transactional model of communication. In J. Akin, A. Goldberg, G. Myers & J. Stewart (Eds.), *Language behavior: A book of readings in communication* (pp. 43–61). Mouton & Co.

Berger, C. R., & Calabrese, R. J. (1975). Some explorations in initial interaction and beyond: Toward a developmental theory of interpersonal communication. *Human Communication Research, 1,* 99–112. https://doi.org/10.1111/j.1468-2958.1975.tb00258.x

Brashers, D. E. (2001). Communication and uncertainty management. *Journal of Communication, 51*(3), 477–497. https://doi.org/10.1111/j.1460-2466.2001.tb02892.x

Burgoon, J. K. (1993). Interpersonal expectations, expectancy violations, and emotional communication. *Journal of Language and Social Psychology, 12,* 30–48. https://doi.org/10.1177/0261927X93121003

Burgoon, J. K., & Ebesu Hubbard, A. S. (2005). Cross-cultural and intercultural applications of expectancy violations theory and interaction adaption theory. In W. B. Gudykunst (Ed.), *Theorizing about intercultural communication* (pp. 149–171). SAGE

Burgoon, J. K., Dunbar, N. E., & Giles, H. (2017). Interaction coordination and adaptation. In J. K. Burgoon, N. Magnenat-Thalmann, M. Pantic, & A. Vinciarelli (Eds.), *Social signal processing* (pp. 78–96). Cambridge University Press. https://doi.org/10.1017/9781316676202.008

Chartrand, T. L., & van Baaren, R. (2009). Human mimicry. In M. P. Zanna (Ed.), *Advances in experimental social psychology* (*Vol. 41*, pp. 219–274). London, UK: Academic Press. https://doi.org/10.1016/S0065-2601(08)00405-X

Clark, H. H., & Krych, M. A. (2004). Speaking while monitoring addressees for understanding. *Journal of Memory and Language, 50*(1), 62–81. https://doi.org/10.1016/j.jml.2003.08.004

Crystal, D. (2006). *How language works.* Overlook Press.

Delia, J. G. (1977). Constructivism and the study of human communication. *Quarterly Journal of Speech, 63,* 66–83. https://doi.org/10.1080/00335637709383368

Dennett, D. C. (2017). *From bacteria to Bach and back: The evolution of minds.* W. W. Norton & Company.

Dragojevic, M., Gasiorek, J., & Giles, H. (2016). Accommodative strategies as core of CAT. In H. Giles (Ed.), *Communication accommodation theory: Negotiating personal and social identities across contexts* (pp. 36–59). Cambridge University Press. https://doi.org/10.1017/CBO9781316226537.003

Epley, N., Keysar, B., Van Boven, L., & Gilovich, T. (2004). Perspective taking as egocentric anchoring and adjustment. *Journal of Personality and Social Psychology, 87*(3), 327–339. https://doi.org/10.1037/0022-3514.87.3.327

Garrod, S., & Pickering, M. J. (2004). Why is conversation so easy? *Trends in Cognitive Sciences, 8*(1), 8–11. https://doi.org/10.1016/j.tics.2003.10.016

Gasiorek, J. (2016). Theoretical perspectives on communication adjustment in interaction. In H. Giles (Ed.), *Communication accommodation theory: Negotiating personal and social identities across contexts* (pp. 13–35). Cambridge University Press. https://doi.org/10.1017/CBO9781316226537.002

Gastil, J. (1995). An appraisal and revision of the constructivist research program. *Annals of the International Communication Association, 18*(1), 83–104. https://doi.org/10.1080/23808985.1995.11678908

Giles, H. (Ed.) (2016). *Communication accommodation theory: Negotiating personal and social identities across contexts.* Cambridge University Press. https://doi.org/10.1017/CBO9781316226537

Hari, R., & Kujala, M. V. (2009). Brain basis of human social interaction: From concepts to brain imaging. *Physiological Review, 89,* 453–479. https://doi.org/10.1152/physrev.00041.2007

Hasson, U., & Frith, C. D. (2016). Mirroring and beyond: coupled dynamics as a generalized framework for modelling social interactions. *Philosophical Transactions of the Royal Society B: Biological Sciences, 371*(1693), Article 20150366. http://dx.doi.org/10.1098/rstb.2015.0366

Hasson, U., Ghazanfar, A. A., Galantucci, B., Garrod, S., & Keysers, C. (2012). Brain-to-brain coupling: A mechanism for creating and sharing a social world. *Trends in Cognitive Science, 16*(2), 114–121. https://doi.org/10.1016/j.tics.2011.12.007

Hewett, D. G., Watson, B. M., & Gallois, C. (2015). Communication between hospital doctors: Underaccommodation and interpretability. *Language and Communication, 41,* 71–83. https://doi.org/10.1016/j.langcom.2014.10.007

Imahori, T. T., & Lanigan, M. L. (1989). Relational model of intercultural communication competence. *International Journal of Intercultural Relations, 13*(3), 269–286. https://doi.org/10.1016/0147-1767(89)90013-8

Ireland, M. E., & Pennebaker, J. W. (2010). Language style matching in writing: Synchrony in essays, correspondence, and poetry. *Journal of Personality and Social Psychology, 99,* 549–571. https://doi.org/10.1037/a0020386

Kim, Y. Y. (2005). Inquiry in intercultural and development communication. *Journal of Communication, 55*(3), 554–577. https://doi.org/10.1111/j.1460-2466.2005.tb02685.x

Knapp, M. L., Earnest, W., Griffin, D. J., & McGlone, M. S. (2020). *Lying and deception in human interaction (3rd Ed.).* Kendall Hunt.

Korkut, P., Dolmaci, M., & Karaca, B. (2018). A study on communication breakdown: Sources of misunderstanding in a cross-cultural setting. *Eurasian Journal of Educational Research, 78,* 139–158. https://doi.org/10.14689/ejer.2018.78.7

Levine, T. R. (2014). Truth-default theory (TDT): A theory of human deception and deception detection. *Journal of Language and Social Psychology, 33*(4), 378–392. https://doi.org/10.1177/0261927X14535916

McCornack, S., Morrison, K., Paik, J. E., Wisner, A. M., & Zhu, X. (2014). Information manipulation theory 2: A propositional theory of deceptive discourse production. *Journal of Language and Social Psychology, 33*(4), 348–377. https://doi.org/10.1177/0261927X14534656

Morelli, S. A., Torre, J. B., & Eisenberger, N. I. (2014). The neural bases of feeling understood and not understood. *Social Cognitive and Affective Neuroscience, 9,* 1890–1896. https://doi.org/10.1093/scan/nst191

Niederhoffer, K. G., & Pennebaker, J. W. (2002). Linguistic style matching in social interaction. *Journal of Language and Social Psychology, 21*, 337–360. https://doi.org/10.1177/026192702237953

Pickering, M. J., & Garrod, S. (2004). Toward a mechanistic psychology of dialogue. *Behavioral and brain sciences, 27*(2), 169–190. https://doi.org/10.1017/S0140525X04000056

Pickering, M. J., & Garrod, S. (2013). An integrated theory of language production and comprehension. *Behavioral and Brain Sciences, 36*(4), 329–347. https://doi.org/10.1017/S0140525X12001495

Pitts, M. J., & Harwood, J. (2015). Communication accommodation competence: The nature and nurture of accommodative resources across the lifespan. *Language and Communication, 41*, 89–99. https://doi.org/10.1016/j.langcom.2014.10.002

Schilbach, L., Timmermans, B., Reddy, V., Costall, A., Bente, G., Schlicht, T., & Vogeley, K. (2013). Toward a second-person neuroscience 1. *Behavioral and Brain Sciences, 36*(4), 393–414. https://doi.org/10.1017/S0140525X12000660

Scott-Phillips, T. C. (2015). *Speaking our minds: Why human communication is different, and how language evolved to make it special.* Palgrave Macmillan.

Shamay-Tsoory, S. G., Saporta, N., Marton-Alper, I. Z., & Gvirts, H. Z. (2019). Herding brains: A core neural mechanism for social alignment. *Trends in Cognitive Sciences, 23*(3), 174–186. https://doi.org/10.1016/j.tics.2019.01.002

Smith, K., Kirby, S., & Brighton, H. (2003). Iterated learning: A framework for the emergence of language. *Artificial Life, 9*(4), 371–386. https://doi.org/10.1162/106454603322694825

Soliz, J., & Giles, H. (2014). Relational and identity processes in communication: A contextual and meta-analytical review of communication accommodation theory. *Annals of the International Communication Association, 38*(1), 107–144 https://doi.org/10.1080/23808985.2014.11679160

Spitzberg, B. H. (1983). Communication competence as knowledge, skill, and impression. *Communication Education, 32*(3), 323–329. https://doi.org/10.1080/03634528309378550

Stephens, G. J., Silbert, L. J., & Hasson, U. (2010). Speaker-listener neural coupling underlies successful communication. *Proceedings of the National Academy of Sciences, 107*, 14425–14430. https://doi.org/10.1073/pnas.1008662107

Taylor, D. A., & Altman, I. (1987). Communication in interpersonal relationships: Social penetration processes. In M. E. Roloff & G. R. Miller (Eds.), *Interpersonal processes: New directions in communication research* (pp. 257–277). SAGE.

Turner, J. C., Hogg, M. A., Oakes, P. J., Reicher, S. D. & Wetherell, M. S. (1987). A self-categorization theory. *Rediscovering the social group: A self-categorization theory* (pp. 42–66). Basil Blackwell.

Zhang, Y. B., & Giles, H. (2018). Communication accommodation theory. In Y. Y. Kim (Ed.), *The international encyclopedia of intercultural communication* (pp. 95–108). Wiley. https://doi.org/10.1002/9781118783665.ieicc0156/pdf

CHAPTER NINE

Contributions and Future Directions

This chapter summarizes the key arguments made in the book, and the contributions and limitations of the framework that we have proposed. We also outline future directions for research suggested by our model, and offer concluding thoughts addressing the practical implications of the perspective we have presented.

At the outset of this book, we argued for the importance of studying understanding; we also argued that the discipline of communication lacks a clear theoretical conceptualization of understanding and a scientific framework that addresses how people achieve it. In the preceding chapters, we have attempted some initial steps toward addressing this gap, articulating a functional definition of understanding, outlining a model of how people create understanding, and discussing how contextual features can influence the processes we outlined. We also briefly addressed theoretical connections to related processes and concepts, including "codes" and codification in communication, deception, expectations, and uncertainty.

Summarized briefly, we have proposed that understanding can be conceptualized as entrainment of communicators' situation models (i.e. multidimensional representations of a communicative episode), to the extent required for communicators' present purposes. We have also proposed that entraining situation models is essentially a process of iterative testing of situation models' predictions against the meme states activated by sensory input, and adjusting and updating situation models to minimize discrepancies.

More specifically, we have proposed that communication can be modeled as a process in which communicators present social stimuli that activate meme states in their interlocutors' minds. Which meme states are activated initially depends on accessibility; contextual stimuli, as well as predictions generated by communicators' situation models, render some meme states more readily accessible than others. Once a meme state is activated in a communicator's mind, it is compared to the prediction offered by the communicator's situation model. If these are generally consistent, the current situation model is confirmed. If this is the case, communicators also tend to presume their situation models are aligned or entrained with their interlocutors' situation models well enough for their present purposes. If there is a discrepancy been the meme state that is activated and the prediction offered by communicators' situation model, communicators experience arousal, which prompts them to take additional steps to resolve the discrepancy. This can occur either individually or interactively, depending on contextual factors. In the process of addressing the discrepancy, communicators revise and update their situation models.

Continuously confirming and updating their situation models to minimize inconsistencies with the meme states activated by sensory input should lead communicators to construct representations of a communicative episode that are (increasingly) accurate depictions of their sensory experiences and the probable causes of those experiences (Friston, 2010). Because communicative episodes are joint endeavors, accurately depicting a communicative episode entails accurately modeling the thoughts and behaviors of all communicators involved in that episode. If all communicators engage in this process in good faith, and efforts at accurately modeling the communicative episode are successful, communicators should all converge on a single, shared situation model for the event. In other words, if this process is successful, communicators should experience entrainment of their situation models.

Three interrelated observations about human cognition and behavior serve as premises for this proposed process model. The first premise is that humans evolved to have a fundamental social orientation; among other things, this enables people to approach creating understanding as a process of using stimuli to activate meme states in others' minds. The second premise is that efficiency is a basic human predisposition; this prompts efforts at optimizing energy use in the meme activation process. The third premise is that prediction is a key mechanism in human mental activity; this is reflected in the central role prediction plays in the process of creating understanding we have outlined. We have also proposed that these observations can help explain the consistent emergence of codified communicative systems ("codes") in situations where people interact with each other repeatedly and share the goal of creating understanding. In this, we have argued that codified systems are not necessary for communication (which contrasts with traditional "code model" depictions of human communication; Scott-Phillips, 2015; Sperber & Wilson, 1995). However, codified communication systems do facilitate creating understanding, and are systematic and predictable outcomes of repeated communicative events.

Theoretical Contributions

We believe that the conceptualizations, model, and perspective on understanding we have proposed offer several potential theoretical contributions to communication scholarship. First and perhaps most obviously, we advance a scientific framework that directly addresses understanding. This includes both an explicit conceptualization of understanding, as well as a proposed process model of how people create understanding. As discussed in Chapter 1, there are many areas of communication research that implicate or indirectly address understanding, such as media effects (e.g. Lang, 2017); health and risk communication (e.g. Desme et al., 2013; Mazor et al., 2010; Stone et al., 2015); humor (e.g. Buijzen & Valkenberg, 2004); and misunderstanding in interpersonal, intergroup, and intercultural interactions (e.g. Coupland et al., 1991; Kaur, 2011; Korkut et al., 2018; Sillars et al., 2005). The framework we have proposed could serve as a unifying theoretical foundation for research in these areas. As discussed in the previous chapter, the framework we have proposed also complements and extends extant theorizing in interpersonal, intergroup, and intercultural communication, among other areas.

Second, the framework we propose integrates and synthesizes research across several disciplines, highlighting consistencies and points of connection between these bodies of work. These points of connection potentially offer a platform for future work addressing both understanding and related topics. We have also grounded our framework in a set of interrelated observations about human cognition and behavior that can be explained in terms of evolutionary psychology. Like all species, humans have evolved to survive in the face of environmental challenges, and it is important to address and account for this in theorizing. With the three premises we outline—that is, that people have a fundamental social orientation, that people have a predisposition toward efficiency, and that predictive inference-making is a basic mechanism of human mental activity—we contribute a set of observations about human cognition and behavior that could serve as a foundation for theorizing on other topics or areas related to communication.

Closely related, we also contribute a model that depicts, and aims to explain, the process of creating understanding in ways that are consistent with the growing body of contemporary research in cognitive science and communication neuroscience. In this, our aim has been to go beyond providing a loose, metaphorical conceptualization and depiction of communication processes (as many traditional models of communication do). As researchers learn more about the biological and physiological processes that underlie people's subjective experiences of the world, we believe it is important to incorporate these findings in theorizing about communication (e.g. Weber et al., 2008). Our framework's conceptualization of understanding as dynamic entrainment of neurological and mental states is consistent with a growing body of neuroscientific research (e.g. Hasson et al., 2010; Nguyen et al., 2019; Stephens et al., 2010). This growing body of empirical research also offers evidence that entrainment includes a predictive component. In their fMRI study demonstrating that brain activity in corresponding areas becomes entrained when people are communicating successfully, for example, Stephens et al. (2010) found that there were some brain areas that were implicated in actively inferring (i.e. predicting) what a speaker will say. Our emphasis on predictive inference-making also draws on, and is consistent with, a robust and growing body of research in cognitive science on prediction as a fundamental mechanism in human cognition, and using Bayesian approaches to model brain activity (e.g. Clark, 2013; FeldmanHall & Shenhav, 2019; Friston 2009, 2010; Hutchinson & Barrett, 2019; Shamay-Tsoory et al., 2019).

Our framework's positioning of prediction as a core process in communication, and by extension, creating understanding, is also a novel contribution in our discipline. While many contemporary communication theories address prediction indirectly (e.g. via constructs of expectations or inferences; see Chapter 8), very little theorizing in the discipline proposes that prediction is an integral part of the process of communication itself. Rather, most contemporary frameworks in communication—even those that move away from a "code model" perspective— depict communication as a process in which people process and then respond to each other's input. Our characterization of communication as a process of prediction, comparison with sensory input, and updating situation models is fundamentally different in terms of the core mechanism it proposes.

To the best of our knowledge, we also contribute an original perspective on codification ("codes") in communication. In advocating for a shift to focusing on the degree of *codification* as a continuum, rather than *codes* as discrete categories, we provide a perspective on communicative systems that more accurately characterizes the range of different ways in which people use stimuli in systematic or patterned ways in different domains. The premises we propose also provide insight into how and why codified systems facilitate (but are not necessary for) creating understanding, as well as how and why codified systems emerge in interaction. We also offer a potential (heuristic) explanation for the degree of codification visible in different systems, which is novel.

A final contribution of our framework is a set of precise conceptualizations and accompanying language for describing aspects of communicative processes that are frequently taken for granted. We offer an explicit conceptualization of *understanding*, and an explanation of how it is created that incorporates both objective and subjective dimensions of the process. We also explicitly distinguish between these dimensions. This offers greater clarity and transparency regarding the nature and process of communication—particularly with respect to how it manifests in a physical world—than do traditional descriptions of "sending" and "receiving" "messages", which do not make such objective and subjective distinctions as explicit.

Limitations

The framework we have presented in this book is intended as a first step, and as such has a number of limitations that are important to acknowledge. First, this framework provides comparatively little detail on the mechanisms by which stimuli activate meme states, how new meme states are created, and how people integrate meme states into situation models. We have sought to provide explanations that are consistent with what is currently known about human cognition. However, we are not cognitive scientists or neuroscientists ourselves, and so our explanations are (necessarily) somewhat abstract and heuristic in nature. This results in two related limitations: first, the theoretical explanations are less precise than we (and surely, some readers) would ideally like. Second, following from this, some aspects of our current framework may not be readily falsifiable, to the extent that we do not specify a precise mechanism to be tested. We see addressing these points as an important direction for future work; we are optimistic that these issues can be resolved or improved in due course.

Creating understanding is a very complex process, and we do not offer a comprehensive model that addresses all these aspects of it, at all possible levels of analysis (and do not attempt or claim to do so). The model of creating understanding we offer is situated at a meso-level of explanation, like much of communication research. Our primary aim has been to outline a model that can be useful to communication researchers, and a model that is as consistent as possible with extant research in other disciplines that does address the cognitive and physiological processes that occur as people communicate. At present, the questions we are not able to address more precisely (e.g. how stimuli activate particular meme states, and how meme states are integrated into situation models) each comprise significant areas of active research, and related debate, in those other disciplines.

Another point we want to acknowledge and underscore is that the key components and mechanisms described in this model are drawn from extant theory and research. In this sense, much of what we have discussed in the preceding chapters is not original or novel in and of itself. The basic arguments that communication is a joint endeavor, and a process of inference-making in context, for example, are well-established and have been for decades (e.g. Sperber & Wilson, 1995). Similarly, the notion of successful communication (i.e. understanding) as entrainment has been addressed and advanced by other scholars (e.g. Hasson et al., 2012), albeit almost exclusively outside the discipline of communication. In the framework we offer, we owe a heavy intellectual debt to scholars like Sperber and Wilson, Pickering and Garrod, Friston, Frith, Hasson, Lieberman and Scott-Phillips, among many others.

However, to the best of our knowledge, the collective body of work we have drawn on, which addresses a range of distinct but related topics, has not been integrated into a single framework, as we have done. Much of this work also has not been addressed in, or linked to, contemporary communication scholarship in the ways we have done. Thus, the contribution we intend to make is not necessarily in any given individual component of the framework we propose, but rather in their integration and synthesis. This model aims to integrate this collection of ideas in a way that is useful for researchers in the discipline of communication, and to bring these ideas to those researchers.

Finally, we also want to acknowledge that there are many other variables that can and do influence human interaction—and thus potentially the process of creating understanding—that we have not included here. Although we provide a brief discussion of some contextual factors that can affect the process of understanding (Chapter 6), we do not address these issues comprehensively or completely, and address only a small subset of possible influences. Closely related, a frequent criticism of models of communication processes in allied disciplines is that they do not adequately account for social factors in interactional processes (Holtgraves, 2002). At present, a similar criticism could be leveled at our framework; we do not offer an extensive discussion of how social goals and perceptions (e.g. impression management, face concerns) influence the process of creating understanding. How additional goals and social factors moderate the processes we outline here, and how they affect creating understanding and related communication behavior, are important directions for future research.

Future Directions

These limitations notwithstanding, we hope that the framework we have proposed both provides insight into the theoretical process of understanding and motivates people to pursue this topic further. We also hope that our framework can serve as a potential foundation and/or starting point for both theoretical and empirical research related to this topic in the discipline of communication. In what follows we briefly sketch some possible directions for such work.

One obvious direction for future research in communication is to study the process of creating understanding. We have proposed a process model for how people create understanding; a next step is to begin testing components of that model. While it may not be possible to test all aspects of the model in its current form, we would encourage researchers to examine the processes and phenomena the model outlines. We see several possible avenues to empirically study understanding, and how people create it.

Understanding can be studied in multiple ways, and on multiple levels. Much of the research we have drawn upon in developing and supporting our framework comes from cognitive science, including neuroscience. Examining how neural entrainment manifests, and is created, maintained, or breaks down under different conditions is one valuable direction for future work. With that said, we recognize that many of the studies we have cited used technology and related resources that are available to only a limited number of scholars in our discipline at present (such as functional magnetic resonance imaging, or fMRI, scanners). They also have significant limitations in terms of the types of tasks they allow. We are optimistic that the development and adoption of technologies that are less costly and more flexible in their use (such as functional near-infrared spectroscopy, fNIRS; for example, Piazza et al., 2020; Sun et al., 2020) may allow more researchers to engage in this kind of work, and may allow researchers to examine theoretical relationships in a wider range of communicative scenarios. Using these approaches will (and does) require that scholars be trained in anatomy, methods, and data analysis techniques that are not currently a part of the standard education that graduate students in communication receive. However, this issue is not insurmountable; there are a growing number of labs in the discipline doing this work, and training students accordingly. We think that communication neuroscience is an important direction for future work in the discipline addressing understanding as well as other topics, with great potential to complement more traditional approaches (e.g. Falk, 2012; Huskey et al., 2020).

For researchers who do not have access to such resources and/or training in neuroscience (like ourselves), there are other ways to study understanding. One avenue is to examine indirect indicators of neural entrainment via behavior and self-reports of cognition. For example, researchers could examine communicative behavior within and across interactions, looking at phenomena like successful versus unsuccessful use of implicature, the extent to which people complete others' utterances, or how communicators' stimuli choices change in response to each other's actions or feedback. Another way to investigate aspects of understanding is to measure processing time or reaction time. For example, our model would suggest that communicators experiencing entrainment should exhibit faster processing and/or reaction times in interaction, because their situation models should provide accurate predictions of what will happen next. Another possible avenue is examining self-reports of people's (conscious) mental states or representations during or following an interaction, with or without additional prompts (as in video-assisted recall; for example, Sillars et al., 2005). These self-reports could then be compared between participants to assess the extent of (conscious) alignment of situation models at a given point in time. (For a more extensive discussion of the importance of dyadic approaches in such research, see Chapter 8).

A related area for future empirical work is studying the development of codified communication systems. In Chapter 7, we have advocated for a shifting our theoretical (and consequently, empirical) focus from "codes" to considering codification as a continuum, and to examining how communicative systems emerge from the process of interaction when communicators share the goal of creating understanding. The explanation of codification as a process that we have proposed can generate testable hypotheses: for example, we would expect stimuli use to change across time, such that less stimuli (and more specifically, a subset of stimuli that constitute the essential feature configuration associated with a target meme state, for a set of communicators) will be required to activate the same meme state later in the interaction. Hypotheses like these can be tested either through a set of tasks with a single dyad, or across multiple dyads that use the stimuli produced by previous dyads, as in iterated learning designs (e.g. Smith et al., 2003). If the iterated learning design was associated with dyadic task accomplishment, we would also expect the process of codification to be calibrated to the demands of the task, such that the degree of codification in a communication system would stabilize at a point optimal for accomplishing the task.

We have also outlined a number of contextual factors that can affect how people engage in the process of creating understanding (see Chapter 6). The effects of these factors are another rich area for empirical investigation. Studies addressing these issues could manipulate and/or systematically test the effects of different levels and/or forms of the variables we have identified: the degree of reciprocity and synchrony afforded by the interactive context; the communication medium; communicators' goals; and cultural or social norms for different groups in interaction. We also see potential to explore and investigate additional contextual factors (as we emphasize that the set of factors we have outlined is far from exhaustive), and their effects on creating understanding. As we have noted above, how additional goals (e.g. impression management) and social factors moderate the processes we outline is an important direction for future research.

Our introduction and integration of the construct of meme states to creating understanding also has implications that could be explored further. As discussed in Chapter 2, this term originates with work by Dawkins (1976), who proposed that memes would be more likely to be replicated, shared, or communicated if they proved valuable to the communicators that host them (see also Dennett, 2017). This suggests that meme states that are useful or valuable to people should be communicated more readily and extensively; we might also expect corresponding patterns of neural activation to become easier to activate for motivated communicators, as they are reinforced through use. These are phenomena that could be investigated empirically; how these processes occur and play out, and their links to the development and evolution of culture, are also potential directions for future work.

Another area for exploration is the potential relationship between understanding, social bonding, and cognitive experiences of reward. There is evidence that when people behaviorally synchronize with others, they experience prosocial outcomes that facilitate social bonding, including perceptions of self-other overlap, perceived cooperation, and activation of the endogenous opioid system (EOS) (Lang et al., 2017). Launay et al. (2016) point out that social bonding is associated with increases in an array of neurohormonal responses, including oxytocin, dopamine, and serotonin, as well as the EOS. Recently, Shamay-Tsoory et al. (2019) have proposed that a single, core neural mechanism might be responsible for multiple forms of social alignment, including synchronization of motor activity, emotional contagion, and social conformity. In their account, this mechanism includes a reward system that is activated when synchronization, or alignment, is successful. Extending such proposals, we suggest that experiencing understanding, a form of cognitive synchronization or alignment, could have similar effects. Thus, another direction for future research is to investigate the relationship between attitudinal and physiological indicators of social bonding, brain activity associated with reward, and people's experiences of understanding.

We also see potential for studying understanding within and across networks of people. As briefly noted in the previous chapter, conceptualizing understanding as entrainment also suggests that a set of people that successfully create understanding can temporarily be seen as a single, integrated, and synchronized system. We see potential for examining both cognition and corresponding communication behavior within and across such temporary systems, including how they form and disintegrate. A related but distinct direction for future work could also be to investigate and/or model how understanding manifests and spreads through social networks as individuals in that network communicate.

Finally, we also see potential for links and integration of the ideas we have proposed in our framework with other theories in the discipline. We provide several examples of links between our framework and extant communication theory in the previous chapter; we would encourage communication scholars to further explore and develop these connections. Additionally, as noted above, there are several areas of communication research in which understanding is implicated, but currently lack a (shared) theoretical framework or foundation that addresses this concept. We believe there is good potential for future work connecting and applying the framework we have proposed here to research in these topic areas, which include health and risk communication, media effects, humor, and miscommunication in interpersonal, intergroup, and intercultural interactions.

Conclusions and Practical Implications

At the outset of this book, we argued that the study of understanding matters for several reasons. First, it is foundational; creating understanding (or difficulty with it) underlies nearly all communicative events that scholars study. Second and closely related, it has implications for research methodology; it is important for researchers to account for understanding in the practices that guide study design and execution. Third, insight into this process may help people make more informed communicative choices in interaction, and troubleshoot difficulties when they arise. Studying understanding, and recognizing that it is an inherently dyadic (or group) phenomenon, may also help people appreciate that creating understanding successfully requires effort from everyone involved in a communicative episode. No single individual is entirely responsible for its success or failure—creating understanding is, by definition, a joint endeavor, entailing shared responsibility (Aune et al., 2005).

As these final points highlight, our framework also offers practical implications for approaching creating understanding in everyday life (in addition to theoretical and methodological implications for communication scholarship). Popular (i.e. lay) views of communication typically locate understanding and misunderstanding at the level of the individual, and ascribe credit and blame accordingly. For example, colloquially, people say things like, "You didn't understand me" or "I don't understand you/what you're saying." This lay conception of understanding reflects the traditional, code model view of communication[1] (see Chapter 1), presuming that people create a vehicle for their encoded ideas (i.e. a message), and ship it to a receiver. The receiver is presumed to then unpack and decode the message; if this is successful, the receiver should end up with facsimiles of the original ideas. When "misunderstanding" occurs, people typically locate that failure in the sender's encoding or receiver's decoding.

Thinking of communication as a process of meme state activation, as we propose, highlights that communicators are *evoking* thoughts or ideas (i.e. meme states) from a pool of possibilities in their interlocutors' minds, rather than taking something from their own mind and dispatching it. This suggests a shift in focus: communicators' primary task is not to package up their own ideas and send them off. Rather, their task is to determine how to activate and/or construct their ideas from what is available in another person's mind. This necessitates thinking about what their interlocutor(s) already have in mind, and adapting the stimuli they select accordingly (to maximize the likelihood that those stimuli will evoke what they intend). It also can entail adapting meme states they seek to evoke, if they think it is unlikely that their interlocutor(s) have a meme available that is similar to the one they wish to call up. In this latter case, communicators must construct their desired meme state (and at a larger scale, situation model) out of what their interlocutors have available. In this, adaptation and adjustment are an intrinsic and inescapable part of creating understanding.

Viewing communication and creating understanding in this way has particularly important implications for situations involving teaching and learning. Thinking of teaching as a process of working with what students already have in mind—rather than providing them with new concepts to process and learn—highlights the importance of meeting students where they are. This includes selecting stimuli—for instance, language and examples—that are accessible and relatable to students, so they successfully activate related content students have in mind. It also includes organizing and presenting material so new concepts or ideas are built out what students have to work with; this perspective thus helps explain and underscore why scaffolding is so critical. Observing the need to adapt teaching to students' needs is not new; however, for us, the perspective offered by our model highlights this point in a new way, and provides an explanation for why it is so important.

Our framework also calls attention to the uncertainty inherent in all communication, and in what we (optimistically) label as understanding. Because people do not have direct access to others' minds, they can never be completely sure that the stimuli they have selected have activated the meme state they intended, or that their situation model is entrained with that of their fellow communicators. This suggests that all communication is intrinsically imprecise, and to a degree, indeterminate. In communicating, people are essentially playing an ongoing social guessing game—an observation that should perhaps give us all some pause, and patience, as we interact with others.

Finally, conceptualizing understanding as a state of entrainment helps us appreciate how communication offers a means of social connection on multiple, interconnected levels. As we discussed in the previous chapter and above, this has theoretical implications for thinking about the social effects of communication. However, it also helps us appreciate the importance of understanding to the human experience. As humans, we are deeply and fundamentally social. Creating understanding is above all a social process and a social achievement, and it has a special importance to our species. While we cannot directly access others' minds, creating understanding allows us to temporarily share, and unite in, the same mental experience. We find this pretty incredible; we hope that, through this book, we have been able to share that.

Note

1. As the preceding chapters make evident, the way we model understanding, and by extension communication, is relatively far removed from a classic "code model" perspective, which was rooted in Shannon and Weaver's (1949) model. However, much of the work in the cognitive sciences that we draw on in proposing an alternative model applies Shannon and Weaver's information theory to model brain activity and brain function. Shannon and Weaver are more relevant than ever to the study of communication, we contend, but not in the way much communication scholarship has addressed their work in the intervening decades.

References

Aune, R. K., Levine, T. R., Park, H. S., Asada, K. J. K., & Banas, J. A. (2005). Test of a theory of communicative responsibility. *Journal of Language and Social Psychology, 24*(4), 358–381. https://doi.org/10.1177/0261927X05281425

Buijzen, M., & Valkenburg, P. M. (2004). Developing a typology of humor in audiovisual media. *Media Psychology, 6*(2), 147–167. https://doi.org/10.1207/s1532785xmep0602_2

Clark, A. (2013). Whatever next? Predictive brains, situated agents, and the future of cognitive science. *Behavioral and Brain Sciences, 36*(3), 181–204. https://doi.org/10.1017/S0140525X12000477

Coupland, N., Giles, H., & Wiemann, J. M. (1991). *"Miscommunication" and problematic talk.* SAGE.

Dawkins, R. (1976). *The selfish gene.* Oxford University Press.

Dennett, D. C. (2017). *From bacteria to Bach and back: The evolution of minds.* W. W. Norton & Company.

Desme, A., Mendes, N., Perruche, F., Veillard, E., Elie, C., Moulinet, F., Sanson, F., Georget, J., Tissier, A., Pourriat, J., & Claessens, Y. E. (2013). Nurses' understanding influences comprehension of patients admitted in the observation unit. *Journal of Health Communication, 18*(5), 583–593. https://doi.org/10.1080/10810730.2012.743626

Falk, E. B. (2012). Can neuroscience advance our understanding of core questions in communication studies? An overview of communication neuroscience. In. S. Jones (Ed.), *Communication at the center* (pp. 77–94). Hampton Press.

FeldmanHall, O., & Shenhav, A. (2019). Resolving uncertainty in a social world. *Nature Human Behaviour, 3*(5), 426–435. https://doi.org/10.1038/s41562-019-0590-x

Friston, K. (2009). The free-energy principle: A rough guide to the brain?. *Trends in Cognitive Sciences, 13*(7), 293–301. https://doi.org/10.1016/j.tics.2009.04.005

Friston, K. (2010). The free-energy principle: A unified brain theory? *Nature Reviews Neuroscience, 11*(2), 127–138. https://doi.org/10.1038/nrn2787

Hasson, U., Ghazanfar, A. A., Galantucci, B., Garrod, S., & Keysers, C. (2012). Brain-to-brain coupling: A mechanism for creating and sharing a social world. *Trends in Cognitive Science, 16*(2), 114–121. https://doi.org/10.1016/j.tics.2011.12.007

Holtgraves, T. M. (2002). *Language as social action: Social psychology and language use.* Lawrence Erlbaum Associates.

Huskey, R., Bue, A. C., Eden, A., Grall, C., Meshi, D., Prena, K., Schmälzle, R., Scholz, C., Turner, B. O., & Wilcox, S. (2020). Marr's tri-level framework integrates biological explanation across communication subfields. *Journal of Communication, 70*(3), 356–378. https://doi.org/10.1093/joc/jqaa007

Hutchinson, J. B., & Barrett, L. F. (2019). The power of predictions: An emerging paradigm for psychological research. *Current Directions in Psychological Science, 28*(3), 280–291. https://doi.org/10.1177%2F0963721419831992

Kaur, J. (2011). Intercultural communication in English as a lingua franca: Some sources of misunderstanding. *Intercultural Pragmatics, 8*, 93–116. https://doi.org/10.1515/IPRG.2011.004

Korkut, P., Dolmaci, M., & Karaca, B. (2018). A study on communication breakdown: Sources of misunderstanding in a cross-cultural setting. *Eurasian Journal of Educational Research, 78*, 139–158. https://doi.org/10.14689/ejer.2018.78.7

Lang, A. (2017). Limited capacity model of motivated mediated message processing (LC4MP). In P. Rossler, C. A. Hefner & L. van Zoonen (Eds.), *The international encyclopedia of media effects* (pp. 851–860). Wiley-Blackwell. https://doi.org/10.1002/9781118783764. wbieme0077

Lang, M., Bahna, V., Shaver, J. H., Reddish, P., & Xygalatas, D. (2017). Sync to link: Endorphin-mediated synchrony effects on cooperation. *Biological Psychology, 127,* 191–197. http://doi.org/10.1016/j.biopsycho.2017.06.001

Launay, J., Tarr, B., Dunbar, R. I. M. (2016). Synchrony as an adaptive mechanism for large-scale human social bonding. *Ethology, 122,* 779–789. https://doi.org/ 10.1111/eth.12528

Mazor, K. M., Calvi, J., Cowan, R., Costanza, M. E., Han, P. K., Greene, S. M., Saccoccio, L., Cove, E., Roblin, D., & Williams, A. (2010). Media messages about cancer: What do people understand?. *Journal of Health Communication, 15*(S2), 126–145. https://doi.org /10.1080/10810730.2010.499983

Nguyen, M., Vanderwal, T., & Hasson, U. (2019). Shared understanding of narratives is correlated with shared neural responses. *NeuroImage, 184*(1), 161–170. https://doi. org/10.1016/j.neuroimage.2018.09.010

Piazza, E. A., Hasenfratz, L., Hasson, U., & Lew-Williams, C. (2020). Infant and adult brains are coupled to the dynamics of natural communication. *Psychological Science, 31*(1), 6–17. https://doi.org/10.1177/0956797619878698

Scott-Phillips, T. C. (2015). *Speaking our minds: Why human communication is different, and how language evolved to make it special.* Palgrave Macmillan.

Shamay-Tsoory, S. G., Saporta, N., Marton-Alper, I. Z., & Gvirts, H. Z. (2019). Herding brains: A core neural mechanism for social alignment. *Trends in Cognitive Sciences, 23*(3), 174–186. https://doi.org/10.1016/j.tics.2019.01.002

Sillars, A., Koerner, A., & Fitzpatrick, M. A. (2005). Communication and understanding in parent–adolescent relationships. *Human Communication Research, 31*(1), 102–128. https:// doi.org/10.1111/j.1468-2958.2005.tb00866.x

Smith, K., Kirby, S., & Brighton, H. (2003). Iterated learning: A framework for the emergence of language. *Artificial Life, 9*(4), 371–386. https://doi.org/10.1162/106454603322694825

Sperber, D., & Wilson, D. (1995). *Relevance: Communication and cognition (2nd Ed.).* Oxford, UK: Blackwell.

Stephens, G. J., Silbert, L. J., & Hasson, U. (2010). Speaker-listener neural coupling underlies successful communication. *Proceedings of the National Academy of Sciences, 107,* 14425–14430. doi/10.1073/pnas.1008662107.

Stone, E. R., Gabard, A. R., Groves, A. E., & Lipkus, I. M. (2015). Effects of numerical versus foreground-only icon displays on understanding of risk magnitudes. *Journal of Health Communication, 20*(10), 1230–1241. https://doi.org/10.1080/10810730.2015.1018594

Sun, B., Xiao, W., Feng, X., Shao, Y., Zhang, W., & Li, W. (2020). Behavioral and brain synchronization differences between expert and novice teachers when collaborating with students. *Brain and Cognition, 139,* Article 105513. https://doi.org/10.1016/j. bandc.2019.105513

Weber, R., Sherry, J., & Mathiak, K. (2008). The neurophysiological perspective in mass communication research: Theoretical rationale, methods, and applications. In M. J. Beatty, J. C. Mccroskey, & K. Floyd (Eds.), *Biological dimensions of communication: Perspectives, methods, and research* (pp. 41–71). Hampton Press.

Index

Language as SOCIAL ACTION ▶

Howard Giles

GENERAL EDITOR

This series explores new and exciting advances in the ways in which language both reflects and fashions social reality—and thereby constitutes critical means of social action. As well as these being central foci in face-to-face interactions across different cultures, they also assume significance in the ways that language functions in the mass media, new technologies, organizations, and social institutions. Language as Social Action does not uphold apartheid against any particular methodological and/or ideological position, but, rather, promotes (wherever possible) cross-fertilization of ideas and empirical data across the many, all-too-contrastive, social scientific approaches to language and communication. Contributors to the series will also accord due attention to the historical, political, and economic forces that contextually bound the ways in which language patterns are analyzed, produced, and received. The series will also provide an important platform for theory-driven works that have profound, and often times provocative, implications for social policy.

For further information about the series and submitting manuscripts, please contact:

Howard Giles
Department of Communication
University of California at Santa Barbara
Santa Barbara, CA 93106-4020
HowieGiles@cox.net

To order other books in this series, please contact our Customer Service Department at:

peterlang@presswarehouse.com (within the U.S.)
orders@peterlang.com (outside the U.S.)

Or browse online by series at:

www.peterlang.com

www.ingramcontent.com/pod-product-compliance
Lightning Source LLC
Chambersburg PA
CBHW050656280326
41932CB00015B/2931